FROM EMACIATED TO EMANCIPATED

The Story of a Skinny Mango

FROM EMACIATED TO EMANCIPATED

The Story of a Skinny Mango

by Captain Ryan "Rev Mango" Althaus,
MDiv, MSBC

Cherish
EDITIONS

First published in Great Britain 2023 by Cherish Editions

Cherish Editions is a trading style of Shaw Callaghan Ltd & Shaw Callaghan 23 USA, INC.

The Foundation Centre

Navigation House, 48 Millgate, Newark

Nottinghamshire NG24 4TS UK

www.cherisheditions.com

Text Copyright © 2023 Ryan Althaus

British Library Cataloguing in Publication Data

A CIP catalogue record for this book is available upon request from the British Library

ISBN: 978-1-913615-98-7

This book is also available in the following eBook formats:

ePUB: 978-1-913615-99-4

Ryan Althaus has asserted his right under the Copyright, Design and Patents Act 1988 to be identified as the author of this work

Cover design by More Visual

Typeset by Lapiz Digital Services

Cherish Editions encourages diversity and different viewpoints. However, all views, thoughts and opinions expressed in this book are the author's own and are not necessarily representative of us as an organization.

All material in this book is set out in good faith for general guidance and no liability can be accepted for loss or expense incurred in following the information given. In particular this book is not intended to replace expert medical or psychiatric advice. It is intended for informational purposes only and for your own personal use and guidance. It is not intended to act as a substitute for professional medical advice. The author is not a medical practitioner nor a counselor, and professional advice should be sought if desired before embarking on any health-related program.

CONTENTS

FOREWORD

We live in a competitive world, and while I am not an expert in the fields of eating disorders or exercise addictions, I do have experience when it comes to competition. I have had the privilege of knowing Ryan for his entire life, and I have followed his journey from a self-proclaimed "kooky" little kid to an elite endurance athlete... and then from an elite athlete to a self-professed "emaciated-anorexic." Now, I am excited to join him on this next chapter of life – quite literally – as he navigates the road to recovery and welcomes you into his story. It is a story that is still being written, and a story that teeters between vulnerability and surrender, strength and weakness, and pride and humility. Most importantly, it is a story that has relevance in the lives of many – far beyond the arena of eating disorders.

It is my hope that reading about Ryan's search for sustenance might help you address and fill any voids that exist in your own life. Whatever your goals are, devote yourself to them and embrace the team around you, because no true champion ever came out of competition unscathed or alone.

Go Ryan!

Bill Belichick, Head Coach of the New England Patriots

INTRODUCTION

Yes, This is Important Enough to Read

Be forewarned! The pages you are about to dive into depict my personal, slightly *disordered* journey with eating, exercise and life. This can be a scary place to visit! Trust me… I live there! As such, I thought I'd offer up a few tidbits of advice (or caution) before you go tiptoeing into my crazy mind.

- **Firstly, and on a practical note:** The time and money spent on a creative writing degree grants me permission to make up words and scribble outside grammatical lines on occasion… or so I claim. Add to that the muddled state of my *malnourished mind* (a term we will dissect in pages forthcoming), and we are bound to bend a few rules of the English language. Thus, I would not recommend reading the proceeding pages with an overly editorial eye, a defensive disposition or an easily offend-able attitude. Instead, read for emotion and enjoy the raw nature of this writing.
- **Secondly:** Take your time! Why? Because, contrary to contemporary culture's misconceptions, we all have time to take. I'll admit, the story to follow might not present as relaxing a read as your average summertime beach book; however, for as difficult as the topic is, I hope that my words remain relevant, and that reading about my journey helps you progress on your own.
- **Finally,** if (or when) you do get triggered, offended and/or confused: Remember that the aforementioned *malnourished mind* has a tendency toward anorexic oversensitivity. So, instead of shutting the book and scorning my shortsightedness when

the subject matter hits a little too close to home, take time to explore what it was that triggered you and why. Allow yourself to *feel* your feelings instead of fleeing from them. *What made you uncomfortable? Where do you relate? Where do you disagree? How can my story be more about you and less about me?*

With all that out of the way, it would seem as though you have two options: You could shut this book and continue about your day while attempting to ignore that elephant named *Ed* who is still lingering in the room... or you could flip the page and dive into my disordered story in the hope that it will help you better you understand your own.

If it is the latter that you lean toward, you might be wondering:

WHO IS THIS GUY, AND HOW'D HE COME TO WRITE A BOOK ON EATING DISORDERS?

Hi. My name is Ryan, or Mango, as those who've experienced my connection to the coveted fruit have come to call me. This a story for another day, but, in short, when mango made its way into my morning meals in an overly obsessive way back in college, my cross-country teammates decided that the funny-looking fruit depicted my personality, skin pigmentation and kooky consumption habits better than my given name did. In the course of the pages to follow, you are likely to learn more about that kookiness than any sane person would ever want to know; however, for the sake of an introduction, here is a brief summary of who it is that is typing the words you are about to read.

At the time of writing this, I am/was a 37-year-old dreadlocked Presbyterian minister, charter sailboat captain and the executive director of a nonprofit program whose mission lies in providing inclusive recreational offerings, intentionally designed to dismantle the faith, social, and economic barriers that divide our community. A *right-coaster* by birth, born and raised in Annapolis, Maryland, I started wandering westward at the age of 18 thanks to a running scholarship that landed me in a little college town just outside of Knoxville,

Tennessee. After a few years of undergraduate work in Appalachian country, I spent the next decade lollygagging around Louisville, Kentucky, where I partook in two rounds of graduate school, all the while trying to make it as a professional marathon runner and Ironman triathlete.

Though the Smoky Mountains of Tennessee and the Bluegrass hills of Kentucky were both beautiful, I was a coastal guy at heart, and the ocean was calling me home. So, upon succumbing to a case of heat exhaustion that left me crawling over the finish line of my final Ironman in 2015, I sold my racing bikes, bought a surfboard and set off for "Surf City," Santa Cruz, California, in an attempt to escape the exercise-centric lifestyle of an endurance athlete in which I was trapped. I was only 32 at the time, but with 65 marathons under my belt, my under-nourished, over-exerted body was broken and begging for a break.

As for my interactions with that disorderly bastard we will be referring to as *Ed*? Well… let's just say that we've had our share of good and bad years leading up to the little landslide that inspired this book. I'll save the details of that relationship for a little later, but in setting the stage for this writing, following a COVID-inspired relapse, I made a choice to take my life back.

That statement sounds pretty proactive; however, in reality, my choice to seek treatment was not so much a choice as it was a necessity, given the slightly more morbid alternative. You see, what I failed to mention was that my stroll down recovery road started – as far too many do – in the intensive care unit, surrounded by a staff of nurses who checked on me every 15 minutes to make sure my heart had not stopped beating. Source of motivation aside, I had made the decision to get better, and despite lying still on that sterilized bed, I had taken a huge first step up the metaphorical mountain that is recovery.

That's all in the past now – and a little heavy for an introduction – so let's close out by focusing on the positives. Recovery was exciting! I was finally going to *get fixed*! I was going to be *treated*! Whatever that meant. I had made a choice to get better, and now someone was going to flip some magic switch on my *mental illness* while I spent a few weeks in residential care restfully relearning the guitar, finishing up the novel that I'd been writing and repurposing my life in *hope* that I might re-enter the real world a bit more peaceful, passionate and plump than I had left it.

Yeah… not quite. For, as Ellis "Red" Redding (played by Morgan Freeman) warned us in *The Shawshank Redemption,* "Hope is a dangerous thing. It can drive a man insane."

Well, insane I became! It didn't take long for me to plummet into the same pandemonium of panic attacks, midday snacktime breakdowns and absurd anxiety that had landed me in the hospital in the first place.

What gives? I wondered, while wallowing in that state of self-imposed disordered eating isolation that we all know far too well. *Where did my laughter and lightheartedness go?* I swore there was a time when I knew how to giggle and revel in life's gaiety. A time when I could go on a date without fear that the French fries in front of me would foil my ability to flirt with the woman seated across from me. A time when I was able to relish in a little R&R without the revolving guilt of skipping a run ruining my reprieve. Simply said, I remembered a time when I didn't take life so stupidly seriously – and upon entering recovery, I was determined to find it again!

Well, the road to recovery turned out to be a rollercoaster ride. I spent 23 hours out of my 24-hour day in anxiety, trying to discern which of the dueling voices in my head to trust as they argued over what I should or shouldn't be doing, eating, thinking, feeling, etc. As for that last hour? That one was spent in anxiety about being anxious! It didn't make any sense! Why did I seem sicker than ever upon deciding it was time to get better? For the lack of more eloquent wording – what the fuck!? Shouldn't my dive into recovery have relieved the inner angst of the disorder? Why was making healthier choices so much harder than making unhealthy ones? And what the hell were "healthy choices" anyway? Shouldn't I have felt better as I popped on a few pounds? Ugh. Furthermore, in a world that whines incessantly about the unintentional ease of weight gain, why was every pound such a painful effort?

Needless to say, this wave of anorexic agony left me in no state to dive in with that bestselling novel I had planned to pen – so I decided chronicle my trauma instead, in the hope that my past and present struggles might help us all scribe a healthier future story.

There you have it. The precursor to the little book that you now hold in your hand: *From Emaciated to Emancipated: The Story of a Skinny Mango.*

Apologies if that was a lot to *digest* – pardon the pun! So, why don't you take a moment or two to catch your breath and reflect on what brought you to read a book on eating disorder recovery; then, when you are ready and raring, I'll meet you on the flip side of the page!

CHAPTER 1

THE ORIGINS OF ED

"Don't handicap your children by making their lives too easy..."
– Robert Heinlein

"... but don't traumatize them by making life too hard!"
– Me

Childhood is *supposed* to be a time when our parents are superheroes, and our imaginations are engaged in the exploration of fantasy worlds... not in fear of the one that we live in. Childhood is *supposed* to be a time when we enjoy eating dessert and dinner *out of order*. Not a time for *disordered* eating! Childhood is *supposed* to be a time when we are happily ignorant to illness – mental, physical or the like. However, childhood is fleeting, and life is not always as it is *supposed to* be. Life is not always fair. Inevitably, we are each destined to reach a point when our youthful obliviousness escapes us, and the doors open for an array of worldly *disorders* to waltz in.

I was a mere seven years old when *Ed* first asked me to dance. True, I had exhibited a variety of cute compulsive behaviors since birth – innocent little idiosyncrasies that made my family giggle. However, one fateful evening, my innocence was corrupted, and all that past cuteness became my future crazy. Up until that time, I had lived the essence of what an American dream childhood was *supposed* to be, or pretty damn close! Our family had 2.5 children (thanks to a half-sister from my father's first marriage), which left us as close to the national average of 2.3 as a family could come without surgical intervention. We had a beautifully manicured green lawn, complete with a chain-link fence that could just as easily have been replaced by white pickets if ever the need arose. I had two loving parents, a carrot-top mop of hair on my head, a basketball hoop hovering over the driveway, family dinner every night, two sisters to tickle me 'til my eyes teared up and a goofy poodle named Scruffy. Yep, I was quite literally living the life that little kids are *supposed* to live.

However, while I was going about my carefree childhood ways, my world was slowly changing and, before long, a cloud of heaviness crept in that cast a shadow on my happy-hearted family. Over the course of several weeks, my mom had started showing signs of increasing stress (despite my not knowing what the word *stress* meant), and my dad had grown strangely aloof. Hell, even the dog developed diarrhea! (Although, in retrospect, this was more likely tied to his habit of eating dirty socks, not the psychological state of my parents.)

Then, one night, it happened. My childhood came to a crashing end. I remember it like it was yesterday.

"Hold still, Ryan!" my mom commanded as she trimmed my toenails over the toilet. "Your squirming isn't helping the situation."

"Ouch!" The scissors had come a little too close for comfort.

Toenail trimming was a dreaded weekly endeavor that only added to the unpleasantries of the conversation that was to come. My fate was sealed. I couldn't escape the words that awaited me because my mother had me held captive by my pinky, but subconsciously, I knew that I wanted to.

"I didn't even touch your skin! You're fine." My mom had seemed a little out of sorts all day, troubled by what, I didn't know. I had brushed it aside, instead spending my time pretending to be a Power Ranger, called to save the world alongside his trusty sidekick, Scruffy the dog; however, I was now in her captivity, and had seemingly lost all my ranger powers.

"Remember when your throat got really sore last month, and everyone took care of you?" She released me from her toehold.

"Yeah…"

"Well, Daddy's sick now, and we are all going to have to try our best to make him feel better." My mom paused to give me the opportunity to respond, but I chose to let silence speak for me. Thus, after a long and awkward pause, she continued. "Daddy's going to be home a little more than usual for a while." I could see that she was holding back tears. "But Daddy is sick, Ryan. So even though he is going to be home a bit more, he can't wrestle or run around with you for a while. We have to let him rest."

Cancer. I didn't know what the word meant at the time – and, in all honestly, I didn't much care about specifics because its subconscious effects had already infected my soul.

My father's doctors dove in quickly to combat his late-stage colon cancer in the weeks to follow, and he responded remarkably well to chemo treatments. So well, in fact, that he took our family on a trip to the Mayan ruins of Mexico. My father was a fighter with a zest for life and a fascination for native mythology, so every time he beat the odds by multiplying the six months that his doctors had originally given him to live, he would take our family on a vacation-styled vision quest as his way of saying "F-U!" to fate.

Mexico was awesome! There were palm tree-lined pools to play in, fish to snorkel alongside and, best of all, bags upon bags of these crazy pink-and-white marshmallows, which tasted ten times better than anything that could be found in an American supermarket! We had been to Mexico twice before by this point, and it had become tradition to stop by the market on the way to our hotel so that my mom, sister and I could load up on snacks while my dad sought out a bottle or two of Central American spirits. Thus, as my father rummaged through shelves of Mexican rum and my mom picked up sandwich-making essentials, I ventured around the aisles of the outdoor market until I found my soft and gooey treasure.

"Bingo!" I grabbed the bag of marshmallows and beelined to find my family. To this day, I still do not know how to say "bingo" in Spanish, but I think it may be one of those universal words. Linguistic lessons aside, I dashed down the aisle, fueled by excitement and guided by glimpses of my daddy's feet as they showed through the gaps of goodies on the shelves that separated us. I careened around the corner at full speed upon reaching the end of the aisle, and then… *WHAM!* I smacked full-force into my daddy's side – right at the stitched-up spot where his chemo pump had been implanted just weeks before.

I remember watching my superhero father fall to the ground. As a child, you aren't *supposed* to see your daddy cry, much less be the cause of it. *Cancer?* I had never understood the word, but I was suddenly struck by the severity of it.

It was in that moment that I first yearned to be small. That I sought to make myself minuscule enough that I would never have to worry about hurting anyone ever again. It was in that moment that I lost my childhood. It was in that moment that the disorder took hold of me – and, from that point forward, I was a danger to myself and the world.

In time, my father recovered from that supermarket slam; however, I never overcame my fear of touching him. I was scared that I would hurt him – I was scared of hurting *anyone*. Moreover, I was scared of myself. I feared the world around me, as well as the thoughts that lived within me, thoughts that I didn't understand. I was scared that the world was out of my control. So, what did I do? I clung to the one thing that I had control over: food.

It started innocently enough. A few oatmeal cream pies and a box of Cap'n Crunch would somehow wind up under my bed after going missing from our kitchen cabinets the day before. I began to build little forts around the house where I'd hoard Tastykakes and hide away for hours on end. I started lining up Skittles on the coffee table, of which I'd consume five – in accordance with their color, of course – during every commercial break while watching SNICK on Saturday night TV. My compulsive absurdities started to take shape in other aspects of my days as well. I began to develop annoyingly anxious ticks, such as swallowing or blinking excessively. Then, when it was time to eat, I began to restrict or binge on certain foods, to the point where my mom once had to warn the neighbors not to "feed the monkey" (her son) because my ten-plus-banana-a-day diet had my pediatrician fearful of a potassium overdose. Yep, shit got weird. I got weird. However, my weirdness was nothing more than a source of comedic relief for a family whose focus fell on a father's worsening condition. *Cancer?* I might not have understood it at the time, but while it poisoned my father's cells, it was simultaneously imprisoning my psyche and soul.

My father ended up passing away when I was 12 years old, following a valiant five-year fight, but damn, if my stubborn disorder didn't stick around. As the years passed by, I did grow out of some of my stranger compulsive behaviors; however, denial and avoidance had become my new norm, and I grew entranced with physical exhaustion and self-induced starvation as easy means of silencing any unpleasant emotions. Throughout the course of my dad's decline, I had developed a deep internal guilt – an emotional angst that I only knew how to combat through physical depletion and/or self-deprivation (i.e., exercise and/or restriction). I would stay outside well after dark, running laps around the yard or shooting basketball until my arms, legs and emotions went numb enough to ignore. I'd regularly have my mom pick me up late from football practice so that I could do a few extra sprints, thus delaying my return to an empty home. Avoidance became my addiction and exercise my means of muting any and all unwanted emotions.

As fate would have it, my dad turned out to be quite the trendsetter, and in the year following his passing, I also lost two grandparents. Three, honestly, because the last living one of the bunch had lost her sanity to Alzheimer's well before we ever lost her to our family. All in all, life was not going as it was *supposed* to go. I managed to finagle my way through the remainder of middle school, despite flailing without a father figure to fall back on, but only because I had become a master of masking my emotions. In that sense, the disorder had already taught me the deadly art of deception.

If things weren't dismal enough upon my entering high school, I kicked off my freshman football season by breaking a collarbone in our first scrimmage. The injury would not have been such a horrible happening, had it not barred me from my last perceivable means of living out the legacy of my football-focused father – the sport that I secretly scorned was all I had left of him. I had always hated football; however, as a scrawny, guilt-laden kid who felt the need to appease their deceased dad, I had pressed onward through the many seasons of misery, only to end up sidelined by an injury at a time when I needed the acceptance of a team the most. I was a failure.

That injury may have ended my fantasy football career, but it turned out to be a blessing in disguise in the weeks to come. Or, as time would tell, a curse *disguised* as a blessing.

"Good God, Ryan!" exclaimed my gym teacher as he looked at his watch during the annual mile run. I had crossed the finish line a full minute ahead of the next student – notably, without the use of my sling-bound left arm. "Have you ever considered joining the cross-country team?"

"But that would mean I would have to stop playing football…" His question seemed conflicted, considering my PE teacher was also the assistant football coach. In reality, we both knew full well that I had "stopped *playing* football" well before ever getting injured; however, that had yet to stop me from spending my afternoons on the sidelines *pretending* to be part of the team.

"That's true." My coach did a remarkable job of looking concerned in his reply. "But as much as we would hate to lose you, you are really fast! The cross-country team would definitely benefit from having you on their squad."

"Really?" It was the first time in my pitiful athletic career that I had ever felt like anything more than a charity case. After all, everyone knew that it was pity that had kept the coaching staff amenable to my uncoordinated occupation of their football field in the first place. "I do love to run… but you really don't think the team would be let down if I left so early in the season?"

"Of course they'd be let down, but no one would ever want to hold you back from a successful running career. Your mile time in gym class alone would put you on the varsity cross-country squad. And that's with a broken collarbone! There's no telling how good you could be if you were trained up and healthy."

That was the beginning of the end. However, as is all too commonly the case with our disorder, the early stages of self-annihilation are often fueled by feelings of relief and elation. Endurance running fed my addiction to exhaustion, and the success I found through the sport fed my ego. This turned out to be a deadly but quite common combination. The feeling following that first skipped meal or first mile run is ecstatic – energizing enough to tempt us to do it again. And we do. This is how an eating disorder is born. That first compliment of one's appearance, or acknowledgement of one's importance, temporarily mutes the voice of our own inner critic by offering an immediate, albeit brief escape that only encourages further restriction, overconsumption and/ or exertion the following day. The disorder not only feels good in its infancy, but it is often praised. As such, we start to need it, and we will honor it in every possible way. *You ran a mile yesterday? How about a mile and a half today? You ate a sandwich for lunch yesterday? How about cutting back on a slice of bread today?* A little more movement, a little less munching. Day in. Day out. Until, before we know it, what started as an innocent diet turns disorderly… not to mention, deadly.

Each of my early anorexic endeavors triggered a feeling of elation and abundance, despite being rooted in depression and depravation, and those false feelings of fulfillment quickly became my reality. They became my addiction – and as is the case with any drug, the addict will strive to elicit the same escape every day following that first high. Unfortunately, that often requires we one-up the previous day's means of achieving it. So, just as a user injects a liquid poison into their veins to address an inner yearning for peace, the anorexic addresses their anxiety through starvation and exertion. Just as the adrenaline junkie seeks solace by climbing up – and often leaping off – ever-rising mountaintops, or as the heart of the businessmen beats based on a decimal point's position on a paycheck, the exercise addict clings to self-exhaustion as a means of freeing them from their inner-guilt. Just as the lonesome lover finds false fulfillment in their latest one-night fling, or the religious zealot encounters the essence of eternity by worshiping a distant deity with rituals they don't fully understand, the anorexic addresses their inner emptiness through… well… *emptiness.*

However, for as ironic – or idiotic – as this may seem in context, let us not focus on our faults so early on in this writing. Instead, how about we take these truths as mere evidence that we are not alone, despite *Ed's* best efforts to make it seem that way.

No. We are not solitary in our struggles. Everyone craves escape, but few ever understand the emptiness they are seeking to fill. Everyone is on a quest to quench some insatiable hunger; however, each individual turns toward a different medium to do so. Thus, our common uniting factor is not that with which we try to fill the void – alcohol, exercise, drugs, food or our restricting any of the above – but the emptiness we seek to fill. Exploring that emptiness is the essential starting point on the path of recovery; however, acknowledging our emptiness is far from easy. Superficial solutions will continue to tempt us by offering up an immediate escape. However, if there was one redeeming quality of an eating disorder, it would be that our addiction forces us to explore this emptiness, literally and figuratively, while most of the world sweeps their unpleasant emotions into the shadows. There are several reasons for this. One is that an eating disorder has physical signs and symptoms that are very difficult to hide. Another is that an eating disorder is far too serious to sweep under a rug. The result? Those who do recover from an eating disorder are some of the most self- and socially aware individuals around. And yes – recovery *is* possible!

I had denied the slow death of my father for years by using food and exercise to control the chaotic world to which his departure had exposed me before I ever worried about my weight. In its infancy, the disorder wasn't about nutrition labels or the numbers on a scale. At eight years old, I couldn't care less about the calorie count of a Klondike bar. I simply knew that I needed to eat one at 7:55pm every Tuesday evening. I wasn't striving to appear skinny or suave when looking in the mirror as I dressed for middle school, but I couldn't help dirtying my shirt while doing push-ups as I waited for the bus, an attempt to burn off the anxiety of an unforeseeable day. I say this to point out that an obsession with numbers, nutrition labels and appearance are merely symptoms of a much larger disorder – and that an eating disorder is but a symptom of an inner emptiness that we do not otherwise know how to fill. So, while symptoms help in diagnosing our disease, treatment must go deeper than the superficial signs of disordered eating if it is to have any lasting effect.

Wow! That was a hella heavy first chapter, but we made it through! Congrats! Now, what do you say we take a break from my story, so that you might reflect on the roots and symptoms of your own ailment? *Are restriction and/or bingeing habits hinting at a lack of intimacy or purpose in your life? Is an exercise addiction your means of running from past trauma and/or present anxiety? Has a purging pattern developed due to a lack of self-worth or a response to inner guilt? What areas of your life are disordered, and what deeper traumas might they have derived from?*

After you've spent some time looking at the symptoms and roots of your unique condition, flip the page and allow me to introduce my esteemed anorexic acquaintance, *Ed*.

CHAPTER 2

INTRODUCING ED

I'll dive back into my story shortly; however, before I do, it is important to acknowledge that this book is not all about me. It is about WE. It is about US and our escapades alongside an asshole named *Ed*. Ed, for those of you who are not on a first-name basis with the bastard, is a *disordered* acquaintance of mine/ours who likes to show up at mealtime or force us to the gym at god-awful hours of the morning in order to isolate us from our friends and family. Yes, Ed, for those blessed not to know him personally, is the personification of our **E**ating **D**isorder. But you are not Ed. You are not your eating disorder!

Now, the fact that you are still reading this little memoir of mine likely places you into one of two categories: Either you found yourself bored in a bathroom or waiting room somewhere and this book happened to be the only reading material within arm's reach, or you or a loved one are experiencing the effects of disordered eating. (That's the politically correct way of saying that *Ed is fucking with your life*… assuming, of course, that there is still such a thing as political correctness in our society!)

Regardless of why you are flipping these pages or how fuddled up you feel your life has become, know that the simple act of opening a book about recovery is a huge step toward opening your heart to it! So, before reading further, pause for a moment and pat yourself on the back. Why? Because in recovery, we celebrate every success, no matter how momentous or minuscule it may seem.

Now, if you are at all like me, neither resting nor reading are particularly easy disciplines to engage in during a recovery dance that is best defined by:

- **An incessant internal struggle to sit still** – I'm a compulsive exerciser with severe ADHD.
- **An incapability to concentrate** – Yet another symptom of a starving psyche, and something that we will delve deeper into in pages forthcoming.
- **An inability to relax** – *Insert anxiety here.*
- **The imprisonment of an exhaustive self-imposed daily schedule** – My obsessive compulsivity, type-A personality and anorexic inclinations converge in creating and implementing in a restrictive and exhaustive self-imposed schedule.

That said, it is my hope that none of these mental health hiccups will hinder your reading because, despite the weightiness of the topic (you will get used to the puns soon, I promise), reading about eating disorders and our parallel journeys to overcome them can be strangely peaceful – permission-giving, even. So, what would happen if you gave yourself permission to be still for a few minutes each day and read in a relaxed state? What would it look like to give yourself permission to rest your body and revive your spirit as you flip through the pages that follow? What would it look like to release yourself from the restraints of your disorder and wade into my words with the intention of reinvigorating your own recovery journey, regardless of what stage of recovery you are in?

If your answer to any of the above is, "I don't know," then how about giving it a try? After all, what do you have to lose? Beyond the lonesomeness of living disordered, that is.

The fact that you are still reading means that you have acknowledged that you have a choice and that you are worthy of exploring and pursuing recovery. You have demonstrated that you have the power to make healthy decisions, so how about you give yourself permission to pause and ponder a more peaceful life?

You're still reading! Great! But before you get too comfy, let me address a few quick issues that might arise in the forthcoming pages and guide you through them now.

- **First,** I am speaking from a personal perspective about the struggles and successes I've encountered thus far on my own journey to overcome an eating disorder and exercise addiction. I am not an institutionalized psychologist who's 20 years removed from the trials, turmoil and tribulations of the recovery process. Instead, I am a vulnerable and passionate partner, trudging through the emotional upheavals of early recovery alongside you. There are plenty of books out there written by individuals who claim to be recovered... and that is awesome! However, when I set off in search of something relevant and reassuring to read while recovering from a recent relapse, I yearned for companionship, not impersonal scholarly scribbles or wistful recollections of someone who had long since distanced themselves from the intense emotions I was experiencing in the moment. I hope that I might be that friend to you. A companion when confronting the crazy compulsivity of our common disorder, as well as a similar-souled sojourner with whom to share in both struggle and success. *Why*? Because companionship is essential if we hope to transform our struggles to successes.
  - **On an ironic side note,** the word *companion* can be traced back to the Latin term *common-panion* – and *panion* translates to *bread*. Thus, whereas a *common* fear of *bread* restricts those living with an eating disorder from many a relationship, let's let our *common goal* to overcome our carbohydrate fears unite us as we wage war against our adversary, anorexia.
- **Second,** there is not one easy means of defining an eating disorder. We each wrestle with different things, are triggered in different ways and live different lives. That said, despite our differences, we each possess a uniquely unifying wisdom – a wisdom which we are called to share with one another. I hope that my writing this while still in the crux of early recovery allows us to address a few of the more isolating emotions that come with recovery so that we might

work through them together. As such, I also want to offer a little encouragement – a simple reminder that, for as dark as the present might seem, not all the emotions that you encounter along the way will be unpleasant. In fact, I have no doubt that you will find that some can actually be quite euphoric! Know that, as you continue along the path of recovery, those pleasant emotions will become more pronounced.

- **Third (or possibly second continued),** this book is about recovery. However, just as there is not any one easily defined disorder, there is no perfectly paved path to it, nor any one definition of what recovery is! My path may not lead to the same "recovery" as yours does, and the obstacles that I encounter along the way might be very different than those that meet you. Regardless of where it is that we are heading, take heart in knowing that our paths are intertwined and that you are never alone on the journey. So, as we dance a bit with definitions in terms of recovery in the pages to come, for the sake of simplicity, let us find alignment in the age-old adage that *the journey is the destination*.

- **Fourth,** it is important not tiptoe around the reality that recovery sucks! Thus, before diving any deeper into it, accept that the prestigious road to recovery is unlikely to be a gleeful gallop through glistening gates of gold with buttercups and bunny rabbits lining the way. Instead, expect an arduous uphill climb that is going to beat the living hell out of you! Take heed, though, because despite the difficulties that will arise, YOU CAN DEMOLISH THIS DISORDER! And no, it is not all uphill. There will be plenty of plateaus and peaceful meadows along the way where you might rest and revive your recovery spirit. Just remember that, when the climb does get intense, no one ever said recovery was easy. After all, if recovery were easy, we would all be recovered – and I wouldn't be writing this book, nor would you be reading it. Furthermore, when you do reach those more peaceful plateaus, avoid allowing yourself to grow complacent in the journey. Be content with the progress you are making and gracious for the life you've been gifted, but also know that the disorder is constantly waiting for us to turn our backs to it. Again, *recovery is a journey*, not a destination, and what makes a journey so beautiful is that never ends.

- **Last but not least,** expect that the journey is going to be scary! Every decision that we make comes with a risk; however, the reward of recovery far outweighs the danger of diving into it. Note the language that I just used: There is an essential difference between something being "scary" and something being "dangerous." Next time your chest tightens, your teeth clench and your heart rate rises upon the mention of a recovery opportunity, you must consistently ask yourself whether the non-disordered option is dangerous or simply scary. If it is dangerous, then, obviously, don't do it. However, if it is simply scary (i.e., recovering), hunker down and have at it!

Alrighty – now that we got that out of the way, flip the page and join me as I reflect on the past two decades of disorderly detours that I took in route to recovery road.

CHAPTER 3

THE SAGA CONTINUES:
CALORIE COUNTING CREEPS IN,
AND ED CREEPS UP

Throughout my sophomore and junior years of high school,
I continued to find fulfillment and acceptance through the sport
of running. My grades were improving, my compulsive behaviors
seemed to be easing, my ego was swelling, and life appeared to be
taking a turn toward what I thought it was supposed to be. I was
juggling scouting visits from NCAA cross-country coaches, a healthy
social life, and a little bit of schoolwork in between. All in all, life –
much like my engagement in the sport – seemed like it was on
track. That was, of course, until something occurred to awaken the
dormant voice of that damn deceiving disorder from deep within me.

It happened one fateful Friday afternoon at the end of my junior
year as I prepared for the State Track and Field Championships.
"You're running well, Ryan," my coach commented as I stepped onto
the scale at the end of practice, "though, I must say, you are a little
heavier than the average distance runner."

Numbers on the scale had never meant anything to me up to that
point, but his pointing them out that day triggered the trauma of my
fateful run-in with my father several years before in that Mexican
market. I can't quite describe the feeling, but suddenly I was overcome
with shame for both my body and my being. I felt disgusted by my
own skin, despite being trapped inside of it, and I was overcome by
an unyielding urge to shrink away to nothing. I yearned to be small –
to be insignificant. At the same time, I felt a deep-seated need to
appease the fatherly figure standing before me, in response to a false

belief that I had disappointed the biological father whom cancer had stolen from me. Skinny. I needed to be skinny. I needed to suffer. And I would starve myself at any cost to do so.

The strange thing about this sudden revelation was that, up until that moment, I had never felt overweight – likely because I wasn't overweight! True, I was a little larger (i.e., stronger) than the average cross-country runner, but it wasn't until I started losing weight that I ever thought I weighed too much. Needless to say, from the day that I first started restricting forward, I consistently felt three pounds too heavy for every two pounds that I lost. Now it doesn't take a mathematician, nor any absurd amount of logic, to recognize that this is not a sustainable pattern for living; however, along with those first few pounds, I also lost my ability to think logically… not to mention, my basic understanding of division and subtraction. The result? A declining high school GPA, and a painstakingly penned book some two decades later about one guy's battle with a rather illogical mental illness.

It has been said by many a therapist that "trauma not transformed is transmitted." I am uncertain who first made that statement, but it was in that moment, as my gaze bounced between the arm of that scale and the eyes of a coach that I would do anything to appease, that the unaddressed trauma of my childhood was transmitted and transposed into numbers. The first few pounds I shed felt amazing! Too amazing, actually, as those early experiences of starvation carried with them an ecstatic effect similar to the feeling of physical exhaustion that I'd used to mask my emotions since childhood. I had found a new means of controlling the world around me and numbing the emotions within, and I was instantly addicted. I remember feeling energized all the time; however, in retrospect, the endorphin rush that was fueling my mania was nothing more than the panicky byproduct of my starving body's search for sustenance. In time, the invigorating energy that self-starvation had once induced started to shift, and I was left debilitated by anxiety. That was okay, though, because I had figured out the simple formula to combat anxiety:

Peace = (Anxiety + Exercise) − Food

Every day I would run a little extra after practice and eat a little less preceding it. A little more exercise, a few less calories. Day in. Day out. And though this pattern would appear to be a death march to any logical onlooker, it seemed like a perfectly sensible and satiating solution to someone living it. Every morning, I would climb out of bed and onto the scale where I would spend my first waking moments staring obsessively at the shiny metal arm as it wavered between markings. It started innocently enough with just a quick weigh-in before breakfast; however, it didn't take long before the size of my breakfasts started to be determined by the direction that the little metal arm would sway. In the weeks to follow, I added a second weigh-in – this one before lunch. And much like my shrinking morning menu, the size of my school cafeteria meal was dependent on the neon numbers that flashed on the PE department's digital scale. That was, of course, before I gave up eating lunch altogether. It wasn't that hard, really. True, those tasty little tater tots did their best to taunt me at first, but after a few days of intermittent fasting, Ed's voice grew louder than the growl of my stomach, and I quickly forgot how to feel hunger.

At 165 pounds, my coach had claimed that I was too heavy, so I dieted my way down to 155 pounds. I felt energized – and I liked it! At 150 pounds, I felt free. And yet, something strange was happening. Physically I was lighter, but my mind, emotions and eyelids began to feel heavy. I started to fall asleep in class and lose my desire to go out with friends. When I hit 140 pounds, something was clearly wrong. I was getting slower. My legs felt stiff and lead-like, and I was sore all the time. I panicked. And panic pushed me to increase my mileage and pull back on the fuel. The numbers continued to spiral downward: 138… 135… 133… 130. I couldn't stop moving, but at the same time, I became too weak to run. I couldn't force myself to eat, but I was starving. I couldn't stay awake, but I couldn't let myself rest. I've come to find that there is actually a scientific explanation for this frantic need to move in response to malnourishment. It is called migration theory, and it describes the body's natural response to restricted food access. In migration theory, the body interprets under-nourishment as a warning sign that we need to seek out new food sources. Thus, the body's metabolism slows in order to conserve the limited calories it has, and we become anxious and restless because our bodies are telling us to migrate (move) to more calorically abundant places.

Migration aside, that little one-liner about trauma – that it is "transmitted if not transformed" – turned out to have significance beyond my fateful conversation with my coach in the weight room that day. It turned out that I was not the only runner to develop an eating disorder as a result of their participation in our high school's running program, and, following several residential treatment trips of his own, that coach was eventually asked to resign from his position. So, if you need a reason to recover beyond your own health, just remember that, while battling an eating disorder is not a trauma that anyone should have to experience, it is certainly not one that any of us would ever want to transmit to another.

I want to acknowledge that I, by no means, blame my disorder on that coach. In fact, to this day, he remains both a valued friend and a fellow traveler in whom I can confide about my compulsive calorie counting and excessive exercise. True, his comments 20 years ago triggered the dormant disorder within me, but they did not create it. I had many teammates who ran their way through all four years of high school without ever once wincing at their weight or skipping a snack. Unfortunately for those of us of who were preconditioned to disordered eating, it was not the healthiest of environments. In recovery, it is essential that we never see ourselves as victims of the disorder, nor use others as scapegoats for our personal struggles. Moreover, it is equally essential that we never feel ashamed, guilty or inadequate for struggling. So, instead of playing the blame game, what if we turned angst about the origins of our disorders into energy to fuel our recovery from them?

In the months between that scale-centric encounter with my coach and summer vacation, I ended up losing a total of 35 pounds… not to mention, any shot at an athletic scholarship, many of my closest friends and any semblance of control in my life. Why? Because I had decided to cling to control of something so superficial as food and exercise instead.

My family had done a fantastic job living a life of denial up until this time, but my condition was becoming hard to ignore – and, as I came to find, the rest of the world wasn't quite as oblivious to my disorder as I had once thought.

"Try one." I remember that first unexpected intervention like it was yesterday, despite the two decades I've spent trying to forget it. My best friend's father had seen me staring at a pack of Oreo cookies on their dining room table one afternoon and offered one up in response. He was a psychologist by trade. As for the Oreos? They were of the Double Stuf variety.

"Huh?" I tried to sound like a nonchalant high schooler, despite my racing pulse and profusely sweating palms. "Try what?"

An Oreo!? My mind swirled with fear. *Is he really offering me an Oreo?! What do I do?! Where do I hide?!*

"I just opened the bag." He calmly made his way toward the table that held the coveted cookies. "I've been snacking on them all afternoon, and I must say, they are pretty tasty." He brought the bag's open edge closer to my trembling hand. "Should I pour you a glass of milk?" His gaze shifted to the fridge and then back to me.

My friend was nowhere to be found at the time. He had gone into his bedroom to talk to his girlfriend and left me all alone in a death match with a bag of cream-filled, calorie-laden cookies – and his sly psychologist father who held them.

My inability to eat that ominous Oreo not only proved to be a one-way ticket to therapy, but it also incited a series of quite uncomfortable conversations with my coaches, family and friends in the weeks to follow. The discomfort of that day wasn't all bad, however, as the added support and supervision that I gained in response did allow me to slow my anorexic slide. Unfortunately, I was not able to crawl back out of the hole I had fallen into on my own.

I managed to tiptoe through senior year with Ed close at my side, but all those precious months that should have been filled with laughter, learning and late nights of stolen liquor remain nothing but a disordered blur. Not because of the aforementioned alcohol, but because my mind was too clouded by anxiety to enjoy or remember them. As far as the athletic side of my story was concerned, after passing out during several practices – as well as at the finish line of our first race – I was asked to surrender my captain status on the cross-country team. Then, come spring, my ego, coupled with my declining athletic performance, forced me to forego track season altogether. I claimed it was because I was bored with competition, but everyone knew the real reason. My muscles had become too atrophied to run, and I couldn't deal with the disappointment I'd bring to the team, my family or myself if I tried. Even prom was a fog, and not because of the typical teenager's beer binge – God knows that there were too many calories in a can for that. I was just more fixated on the dinner that my date had demanded we share before the dance than on my actual date.

> Dear date (you know who you are),
> I apologize for failing to tell you how great you looked that night. I promise that I'll give you a call once I figure out how to do dinner in a non-disordered way. Maybe then we can try things again?
> With Love,
> Ryan**

**I may not be an Eaters Anonymous guy, but I do know that several of the 12 steps focus on making amends to those we've hurt. So, as I work to overcome a disorder defined by guilt, an apology some 20 years late seems like a good idea.

CHAPTER 4

ED'S IDIOSYNCRATIC (OR IDIOTIC) INFLUENCE INTENSIFIES

"This milk tastes strange." My sister looked up from her bowl of Cheerios one morning with a hint of accusation in her eyes. "It's really sweet." Her gaze shifted toward the milk carton before landing on yours truly. "Did you do something to it, Ryan?"

"Sweet? No. I don't even drink milk," I said in my defense, despite knowing damn well that I had dumped sugar into the carton before she had woken up. "Why would I mess with the milk?" Although it was seemingly directed at my sister, my question was actually pointed at myself. *Why would I mess with the milk?* It was the strangest thing – and I couldn't keep myself from doing strange things. For weeks I had kept a small carton of soy milk (the lite variety, of course) on the side shelf of the fridge for my own sipping, while simultaneously sweetening the regular milk that my unsuspecting family savored.

So, why would I pour sugar in the milk? Because it felt strangely soothing to watch my family drink a few extra calories while I cut them from my diet. And my weird ways didn't stop with the milk! I began to hide and hoard food all around the house – a strange action, indeed, for someone whose obsession lied in not eating. Worse yet, I am embarrassed to admit that, on more than one occasion, I even stole snacks from the grocery store, despite having grown up an honest kid in a home where the pantries were never bare. I began to prepare elaborate meals for my family every evening, but I would never eat my own cooking. Slabs of steak sautéed in butter alongside dressing-drenched salads, topped with croutons and cheese. Bon appétit! Meanwhile, I'd steam some veggies up with a dash of salt and pepper as a complement to my main dish: a plate of lettuce with a sprinkling of balsamic vinegar and a slice of smoked salmon. In other words, the strange obsessiveness that I'd exhibited toward food throughout my younger years had not only returned, but the ritualism of my past had evolved into restriction and made me a helpless observer to my own anorexic idiosyncrasies. Things were not looking good. At least as a kid I would eat the bizarre foods that I prepared – even if that meant ingesting ten or more bananas a day. Now, I couldn't even get myself to peel one out of the fear that my favorite childhood fruit was too laden with carbohydrates to consume. I was absolutely out of control in my quest for control and, as such, completely controlled (and not to mention confused) by my own crazy compulsions.

As my kooky culinary rituals continued to intensify, I came to find that my friend's therapist father – the bearer of Oreos – had been collaborating with my mother in recruiting a psychologist who specialized in eating disorders. Needless to say, their intervention was not one of discussion, but demand; so, after a tiny teenage temper tantrum, I conceded to counseling. If I didn't already feel like enough of an outcast amongst my friends or an awkward visitor in my own body, I was now officially a psych case – a designation that did wonders for my deteriorating self-esteem.

This wasn't my first go at counseling. I had been to a therapist once before when I was nine to talk about my dying dad; however, those childhood psychology visits had never proven to be much more than overpriced supervised coloring sessions. So, whereas I did not fully know what to expect during that first session some six years later, the confidence that I had developed in my disordered trickery, coupled with my past counseling experience, assured me that I would be able to convince this woman that our visits were a waste of time.

"Good afternoon, Ryan." Her voice was about as crisp as the steam-pressed suit that she sported, and before giving me a chance to return the salutation, she dove right into the heart of the disorder. "Tell me, before we get going, how much do you weigh?"

"Huh?" No superficial small talk or cordial greetings. No "how are you doing?" or "how are you feeling?" She simply hit me head on with that awkwardly unsettling question.

"Um. I don't know… 150 pounds or so?" Having already weighed myself three times that day, I knew the answer quite well. I also knew that the real answer would not help my situation, so I innocently rounded up about 20 pounds to pacify the woman perched perpendicularly to my seat.

"Bullshit." If her initial question hadn't caught me off guard, her response to my answer certainly did! A wave of fear washed over me as she proceeded to pull a scale out from under the couch. "How much do you weigh, Ryan?" she asked once more.

"I'm not sure. I don't have a scale." *Besides the one in our cross-country locker room, the one in the upstairs bathroom of our house and the one hidden under my bed, that is.*

"No worries. Why don't you just hop on mine and tell me what it says."

It would be a stretch to call my movement a *hop*, but I slowly crawled onto the scale's metal surface and mumbled out the neon numbers on its screen. "One hundred and thirty-two pounds."

"That's with shoes and clothing." She paused. "It would seem as though your original guess was a teeny bit high now, wouldn't it? You probably don't want to pursue a career as one of those guess-your-weight guys at the amusement park any time in the future."

"Yeah, probably not." I squirmed awkwardly on the couch while she gazed into my eyes. She was studying me, and I felt like I was failing her test. I always felt like I was failing.

"I'm curious, Ryan. Amusement-park employment aside… do you want a future?" She smiled encouragingly, despite the serious implications of her inquisition.

That question has haunted me for nearly 20 years. *Do I want a future?* Of course, I wanted a future. Like many of you reading this book, my eating disorder was *supposed* to be just a phase. A little bump in the road. Something that I would grow out next month… or next year at the latest. Never would I have expected at age 17 that I'd still be dancing with some disorderly dude named Ed two decades down the line! No, had anyone told me at age 17 that I'd be doing a second round of inpatient treatment at age 36, I would have broken out in laughter. Hell, at that point, I would have scoffed at anyone who told me that I was preparing for a *first* trip to the hospital while sitting in that therapist's office. At that time my eating disorder was nothing but a phase. There was no way that I'd be spending future decades fretting over French fries or fudgesicles. That would be absurd.

Well, the reality of an eating disorder is that it doesn't just go away – and ignoring it in hope that it will is, indeed, the greatest of absurdities. If we want to be free from our disorder in the future, we must start fighting for our freedom in the present... like, as in, today! Welcome, my friends, to your future.

Interestingly enough for all you fellow nerds, there is actually an entire philosophical school of thought known as absurdism, which is based on the existentialist views of Albert Camus and proves relevant to our conversation today. As Camus famously remarked, "Man is the only creature who refuses to be what he is." Never has that statement been truer than when dealing with a *disorderee* who refuses to accept how they look, the weight that their body wants to weigh, or the ways of the wacky world in which they live. In response, we cling to control of the things that we can influence (such as the calories we consume and/or the ways we rid ourselves of them) in a futile attempt to claim control of an otherwise crazy existence. Absurd, indeed!

Fast-forward with me through a summer of therapy alongside that no-shit-taking shrink in preparation for my college send-off. I had lost all but one of my scholarships by that point; thus, the only option I had left was a small Division III college on the eastern shores of my home state of Maryland. It was close enough to appease my therapist, whom I had spent the better part of my summer convincing that I was healthy enough to attempt life on my own, as well as my mother, who even agreed to let me join the college's cross-country team, under the condition that the training staff would monitor my weight weekly. So, that was it. I was going to give life a try!

I want to pause here to acknowledge some of the more enjoyable, non-disordered aspects of life during that time. Why? Because contrary to how it can feel while deep in the throngs of those dismal disorder days, life is actually larger than our eating afflictions! I was able to find a little reprieve that summer exploring the Chesapeake Bay as a youth sailing instructor while working hard to reconnect with a few of the friends who I had pushed away in the preceding months. I even adopted an amazing dog, Kaya, who would come to serve as a trusty first mate on my boat and best buddy on long walks for many years to come. It was also during those sunny summer days that I began to notice another rather unexpected consequence of those long hours spent in introspection. The struggles that I had been working through, and the coping methods I was learning to help in that process, had made me much more mindful than most teenagers. In response, I had developed a mindfulness and emotional awareness that far surpassed that of my peers. I started to savor sunsets and would periodically pause in appreciation of flowers I passed. I was becoming much more attentive of the otherwise unassuming aspects of life that most teenagers remained oblivious to, and I was exploring emotions that I'd never before allowed myself to feel. On a practical level, my need to stay active, coupled with my propensity to be productive, kept me from wasting my days away binge-watching bad TV or sleeping past noon. I worked hard to cut back on exercise, and this awarded me ample time to pick up a few new hobbies, such as gardening and painting. When I did eat, I did so in a mindful way that allowed me to actually taste what it was I was eating – something we often forget to do in our grab-and-go Western world. So, whereas life during this time was not exactly *easy*, it wasn't all bad either. I felt it important to include this more positive paragraph as a means of reiterating just how essential it is to soak up some of the non-disordered aspects of the life that you are living while plodding along the path of recovery. Or, should I say, as a subtle reminder that you can still live your life while working to figure out how to live in a less disorderly way. Find an identity outside your eating disorder instead of allowing your life to be defined by it because you are more than your disorder!

College kicked into gear that fall, and though it wasn't easy, I managed to make it through most of my freshman cross-country season without straying more than two pounds to either side of my minimum requirement. As for the rest of life, I was able to maintain a moderately healthy balance between my schoolwork, my social life and my athletic pursuits. In fact, as it turned out, my obsessive tendencies acted to my advantage academically, and my studies as a biology major began to open my eyes to the broader science behind my body and its need for fuel in order to function. So, again, was college easy? Not at all! I remember waking up freezing every morning and forcing myself out of bed so that I could swim a few laps in the student center's pool or put in a few sunrise miles before 8am lab. I can still feel the awkwardness of my many failed attempts to strike up a conversation with the cute girl from chemistry class. I attempted the dating thing a time or two; however, after a few failed flings, I gave up on finding a girlfriend who didn't mind sharing me with a jealous dude named Ed. As for food? My stomach still flips when I envision the school's surprisingly decadent dining hall. I was too uncomfortable to eat publicly at the time, so I had to get special permission to bring a to-go box with me. That way, I could sit around and be social for a while before retreating to my room, where I could eat in isolation, without the overwhelm of looking at endless buffet tables. I have found that being around either too much or too little food creates a lot of anxiety because I've always struggled with the thought of anything going to waste.

"Um… I've got a lot of food allergies," I'd respond when asked about my abstinent dining habits.

"Oh, that sucks. Which foods?"

The ones that you eat, I'd say to myself. This was actually kind of true. Over the years I had developed a strange allergic reaction to anything edible outside of lettuce. A nauseating response to the aforementioned anxiety… and food made me anxious!

So, no. Freshman year was not a particularly easy experience. But freshman year isn't *supposed* to be easy for any teenager. I am just happy to admit that, despite it not always being gleeful, the year wasn't completely disordered either. At least, until a fateful cross-country practice when…

"Lift up your shirt, Ryan."

Panic! I had been caught. My cover was blown… literally! A wave of guilt flooded over me as I slowly lifted my shirt to reveal the five-pound weight that I had taped to my torso.

"How long have you been doing this?" the trainer asked with disappointment in his eyes. My silence told him that I wasn't ready to let him in on my little secret, so, after a very long and lonely moment, he commanded, "Come with me."

The cold concrete walls made me feel like an inmate marching toward the electric chair as we weaved through the hallways of the athletic department. I remember the nauseating panic that met me as we rounded the corner in approach of the cross-country office's open door. "Would you like to tell him, or should I?" the trainer asked in a voice plenty loud enough to elicit my coach's attention.

"I… um…" I had known the consequences of my actions before ever taping that weight to my back; however, having weighed myself earlier that morning, I also knew that I wouldn't have been able to compete in our regional meet that weekend had I not acted. (My typical approach of water-loading before weigh-ins wasn't going to cut it that day, and my roommate was starting to get outwardly annoyed by my many nightly pee-ventures. "I feel like I'm sharing my room with an 80-year-old man with a case of *prostate elephantitus,*" he half-jokingly said early one morning, before personally offering to pay for a catheter.)

"He had this taped to his back, Coach." The trainer held the iron plate out in his hand.

"That would explain your declining performance in practice lately, Ryan."

I'd been struggling to keep pace with the pack as of late and, to make up for it, I would punish myself by running a few extra miles after practice every day.

"We had an agreement, Ryan. You know what this means."

I was overcome by a wave of panic. *Who am I if I'm not an athlete? What am I if not a runner?*

That day not only marked the end of my cross-country season, but for all I knew, it marked the end of my athletic career altogether.

The remainder of that year was a rollercoaster ride full of ups and downs, curves and crevices, and anxiety and depression. With every step I took, I felt as though I was tiptoeing across a tightrope over a roaring anorexic avalanche – and there was no safety net. I needed to make a fresh start if ever I hoped to reclaim my life and, in response, I managed to pull myself together just enough to earn an academic scholarship at a little Christian college in the foothills of Tennessee.

I was not a Christian at the time, and the only thing I knew about Tennessee was that moonshine gave me migraines, but neither of those things mattered very much, so I packed up my Nissan Pathfinder, signed up for a country line-dancing class and set off on a southbound adventure. Following my dishonorable discharge from my last school's cross-country program, my athletic expectations were low upon arrival; however, I was elated to receive an invitation to walk on to their team. Furthermore, the gratitude I felt in being given another chance was motivation to get myself healthy and stay honest.

As a condition of moving away, I agreed to meet with an eating disorder specialist once every week, and following every practice, I was required to check in with the athletic training office so that they could monitor my weight and heart rate. I had made a commitment to my coaches, family and therapist to challenge my eating disorder, and though taking on anorexia and academia all at once made for an arduous first semester, it proved to be a moderately successful one. Unfortunately, as positive as my intentions had been, I had yet to make a commitment to the most important person: myself. Thus, when I found myself with a little more free time and a little less accountability at the climax of cross-country season that fall, I started to slip. (Actually, upon re-reading my own writing, I feel that the word *slip* might be a bit of an understatement – let's think of it more as a *slide* into a *tumble*.) I ended up losing more than ten pounds in the three weeks spanning regional cross-country championships and my final exams – not to mention, a few points on my GPA and any semblance of sanity that I had been clinging to throughout the season. Little did I know that, as I bullshitted my way through my physics final, the real test was waiting for me at the door of my Maryland home.

"Not a chance!" I yelled in response to my mother's not-so-cordial greeting. "There is no way I am going to a psych hospital! I'm fine!" A wave of emotion – one far too intense to discern what it was that I was actually feeling – had crashed over me. I had been deceived by my own mother and was now left floundering for words in a sea of fear. I wasn't scared of treatment, per se. I was scared because I knew the truth: I wasn't fine. I was sick. I was disordered... and my attempts to claim otherwise were not fooling anyone.

I would later come to find that my mother had continued to see my original eating disorder therapist long after I left for college, and that the two had been plotting this little welcome-home intervention ever since receiving a call from the college's training staff a few weeks prior to my return. They had told my mom that I had stopped checking in and appeared to be losing weight. Thus, with that call, and a little encouragement from my/our therapist, my mother arranged for me to go for an intake evaluation at Shepherd Pratt, an intensive eating disorder program in Baltimore, Maryland, the following day. I knew in that moment that I couldn't escape my fate, that, despite any outward showing of opposition, I was going to be institutionalized... and I also knew deep inside that was exactly what I wanted.

My mom fell silent as the tears rolled down her cheeks, and, though I am sure she did eventually respond to my abrupt declaration, I was too angry to remember what she said. I wish I could say that I was mad at her in that moment, but as hard as I tried to turn my anger outward, it was derived from and directed within. The truth was that I was mad at myself. I was mad at myself for needing an intervention. I was mad at myself for bringing my own mother to tears. I was mad at myself for crying, which I had also begun to do. I was mad at myself for existing... and I was mad at Ed! So, no, I wasn't mad at my mother for speaking up. I was angry because I had known the truth before she ever had to open her mouth. And the truth was, I was not fine. Thus, I was angry because I knew what I had to do, and it was a far cry from how I had planned to spend my winter break. Actually, I wasn't angry at all – I was scared. Terrified! And fear is anger's sinister sister. I was scared because I knew that I was out of control, and that the only thing

I could do about it was surrender control. I retreated to my room that evening and slammed the door behind me, not to show my face again until morning. Yep, I was petrified – but pretending to be pissed off.

The next day, I remained hidden under the covers until I heard my mom leave for work. I could not stand to look into her worried eyes. Thus, I breathed a sigh of relief when I finally heard the car's engine roar to life, and I slowly rolled out of bed as it rolled out of the driveway. Then, after a quick swig of water, I laced up my running shoes and dashed out the door to do what it was that I did best, figuratively and literally: run!

I ran and I ran. Then, I ran a little more. I didn't run fast; after all, I had surrendered that ability, along with any remaining muscle mass, over the course of the previous month. However, I ran with purpose. I ran to escape the emotions that had kept me awake all night, and I was fueled by the fear that all those feelings might catch up to me. But then, a few miles into my asphalt escape, something strange happened. All of a sudden, I got tired. Physically, yes – I was sleep deprived, malnourished and over-stressed. This was nothing out of the ordinary. I had become an expert at pushing past physical pain and fatigue by that point, so there was nothing strange about the feeling of lead in my legs and eyelids. But I also had a new cause for exhaustion, and it was all emotional. I was done. I was tired of avoiding my afflictions. I was tired of punishing myself. I was tired of pushing myself, mile after miserable mile, across the hard concrete surface of my self-imposed prison. I was, quite simply, tired. Exhausted, actually – and in response, I turned around. It was in that moment that I made a choice to stop running *from* my problems and start running – well, hobbling or crawling by that point – *toward* a solution. I was too emotionally overwhelmed to realize the significance of the situation unfolding, but in retrospect, it was in that instant that I first acknowledged that I had a choice. I could talk back to the disorder.

By the time I got home that morning, I was drenched in a salty mixture of sweat and tears, but filled with an exhaustion-induced, yet strangely energizing clarity.

"I'm ready… let's go!" I yelled as I barged into the kitchen, startling my unassuming sister before she could finish her breakfast.

I had packed my bag the night before during an episode of insomnia because, though I was uncertain at the time whether I would need it, I knew that if I could build up the courage to commit to recovery, it wouldn't likely linger very long.

"Let's go," I repeated. We needed to leave before I had the chance to change my mind. We needed to leave before the fear that I had left out there on the road that morning could catch up to me. We needed to leave before my mom came home because I couldn't handle seeing her cry again. We needed to leave – quickly!

"Um, okay…" My sister sat there studying her sweat-laden, broken brother. "But… where are we going?"

We were in the car heading to the hospital before I could catch my breath, and while the next 48 hours remain but a blur of blood pressure cuffs, beeping machines, needle pricks and forced feedings, I'll never forget the bliss that came in knowing that I wouldn't have to wake up alone with Ed the next morning; the bliss of knowing that I would not have to painstakingly lace up my running shoes with fumbling fingers and a foggy mind for the next few weeks; the bliss of knowing that I would not have to forgo food all afternoon while my stomach screamed of starvation; and I would not have to fear that my heart would stop beating during my morning workout because I wouldn't have to force myself to work out! Finally, I'll never forget the freeing feeling that filled my soul as I thought about not having to spend another evening deep within the throngs of anorexic isolation. It was simultaneously one of the most painful and pleasurable experiences of my life – and as strange as it sounds to say, what I would come to find was that it was within the confines of that psych unit that I first tasted freedom. And, along with the powdered mashed potatoes that somehow managed to make it onto the menu each day, I liked it!

CHAPTER 5

EXPLORATIONS OF EMOTIONAL FREEDOM THROUGH PHYSICAL IMPRISONMENT

Wake-up calls started at 6am, and upon opening my eyes that first morning and expecting the dream would be over, I was surprised to find a scrub-clad nurse standing beside my bed.

"Good morning." The nurse smiled as she fiddled with the twisted wires of a rolling EKG machine. "Mind if I check on that heart of yours? Your low pulse rate caused a bit of a stir with the night staff last evening. So, what do you say we start the day by making sure you are beating, breathing and ready for breakfast?"

"You're the boss," I replied, squirming under the stiff, sterilized hospital sheets. I untied the gown that would serve as my morning, afternoon and evening attire for the month to come, and then cringed when the cold gel hit my exposed chest.

"While we are at it, I'll also need to draw some blood and prick a finger for a glucose reading." Had I known at the time just how badly bruised my fingers would be by the end of that five-week stay, I may have flipped her a different finger than the one I offered; however, a sore pinky paled in comparison to the pain that I had inflicted on myself back in the real world.

Over the days to follow, I came to enjoy the companionship of my slightly psychotic fellow patients, as well as the routine nature of the hospital. (I do have obsessive compulsive disorder, by the way.) I quickly befriended the nurses who would greet us every morning for weigh-ins, check our vitals, send us to shower and sit with us for breakfast. After breakfast, we would meet for group therapy to discuss silly things, such as the stress induced by the syrup-soaked sausage-and-pancake platter that morning, as well as more existential topics, such as the purpose of life in and beyond treatment. Following group therapy, we would gather for some sort of activity, such as an art project, mindful movement, music therapy or the like. Then came snack time. Snack was followed by free time – though I use the term "free" very loosely. Before we knew it, lunch would sneak up on shiny silver carts and cast a wave of panic over the room as we would each painstakingly plod our way to the tables. Following the meal, each resident had the chance to meet one on one with their psychiatrists, psychologists and social workers. (And if you are reading this and you don't know the difference between a psychiatrist, psychologist or social worker, CONGRATULATIONS! You're living a great life!) Following our individual appointments, we would dive in with a mid-afternoon snack, a second group session, a little arts and crafts, dinner, some more not-so-free time and finally, one more snack before bed. Day in. Day out. Monday bled into Tuesday. Tuesday faded into Wednesday. Wednesday somehow turned into Saturday, etc., etc., etc.…

Having come out of such an intense state of emotional chaos, the routine nature of the hospital was somewhat soothing; however, as my anxiety started to slow, I came to appreciate little variations that would break the monotony of the day. I began to look forward to visits from my friends and family, as well as special activities such as yoga or a fresh-air field trip to the courtyard. Journaling became a passion of mine, and I began to utilize art as a means of expressing the many past and present emotions that I was exploring alongside my psychiatrist, a middle-aged man with an exotic accent that complimented his equally interesting tie collection. I took comfort in the ease of decision-free living – so much so that I began to develop a fear of the world that I knew was lingering outside of the treatment center.

"What is the purpose?" I remember asking, during one of my favorite weekly meetings.

"The purpose of what?" The hospital chaplain looked inquisitively into my eyes. She was in her mid-40s, and although she was Christian by creed, she consistently opened the doorway for me to discuss my doubts surrounding all faith traditions. I pause to acknowledge that I am writing this nearly 20 years removed from these interactions and am now an ordained Christian minister who served as a hospital psych chaplain during seminary. Nevertheless, let it be known that, despite eventually earning the "Reverend" title myself, I was an anorexic agnostic with plenty of questions about God, Buddha and the like. (FYI: Even now as an ordained minister, I still have a lot of doubts and even more questions. So, I have yet to discover any definitive answers in terms of divinity, but I have learned that doubt is a key component of faith – because faith is about trusting... not knowing.)

"What's the purpose?" I asked once more.

Oh, and let it also be known that agnosticism is not the absence of a belief in God – that would be atheism – literally "a" (no) and "theos" (God). And though I dance with that one too on occasion, agnosticism is simply the admittance that we do not know. The word, when broken down to its Greek roots, literally means "a" (not) and "gnostic" (know).

"Want to be a little more specific?" The chaplain's voice was calm, playful even. She had obviously been asked this before.

"Eating. This place. Life. What's the purpose of it all? What does it all mean?"

"Ha!" she chuckled. However, what she said next would not only stick with me for nearly two decades, but I am confident that it will continue to guide the many more years I hopefully have left to live.

"The purpose of life," she answered, "is to find purpose in living."

This simple phrase reminded me why I had entered treatment in the first place – and why I would soon need to step out of the residential bubble and re-enter the real world. It also set me on a quest to find a source of fulfillment in my life beyond the three well-balanced, meals that I'd become accustomed to eating each day. Throughout the years proceeding that chaplain's prophetic proclamation, I had used my eating disorder as a means of hiding from life – a means of pushing aside my grander purpose. Why? Because, like many of you, I was scared to pursue my potential. I still am, and with good reason. To commit oneself to their pursuit of purpose means taking a leap into the unknown – a leap that comes with the risk of failure, rejection and vulnerability. An eating disorder, on the other hand, feels safe. It is a means of clinging to control (or the perception of such) and hiding behind a veil of victimization and weakness. It is also a distraction – a temporary means of addressing the empty spaces in our souls. However, sitting with those empty spaces in the days to follow our conversation allowed me to start accessing life… life beyond Ed. What void was I seeking to fill with food (or the lack thereof)? I'm still working on the answer to that, but to jumpstart the journey, upon returning to college that spring, I proceeded to drop my pre-med major and take a dive into the metaphysical (beyond-physics) world of the humanities. The chaplain's words had evoked an evolution within me; however, in retrospect, I must admit that my decision to reroute my career path was also heavily influenced by the fact that I was the only pre-med student in my class who passed out every time they saw blood.

Our conversation on purpose not only put me on a path to attain dual bachelor's degrees in English and theology, but also paved the way for several years of graduate work in theology and philosophy, as well as an eventual career in ministry that included serving as a hospital psych chaplain. And though I wasn't ready to accept any one religion at the time, nor surrender the many doubts I held about religion as a whole, her reflection had sparked a curiosity that would forever redirect my life. Thus, I set off on a mission that day, not to understand "the purpose of life," but to "find purpose in living it."

I want to reiterate that the reason I am writing this book is because I do not believe, nor can I accept, that our eating ailments and disordered diagnoses are the end of us. We must trust that the adverse experiences we encounter throughout the course of our lives are what grant us the wisdom necessary to help one another. We have to believe that the obstacles we face along the way are never meant to isolate us; instead, they're supposed to guide our personal and communal evolution. We must not let our struggles break us down or make us feel disordered because they are opportunities to grow stronger and expand our capacity for empathy. In that regard, I've always found comfort in the age-old adage, "God will never test us with more than we can handle." Why, you may wonder, does that resonate? Because, if that statement is true (which I wholeheartedly believe it is), God must think that us ED folk are pretty freakin' badass. Lord knows we have been given one hell of a test – or opportunity!

To this day, I still cling to my "a-gnostic" (un-knowing) roots, despite my clerical career choice, but what I *do* know is that we awaken every morning with a choice between seeking meaning in living, or mindlessly going through the motions of mundaneness. We can elect to pursue freedom from our disorders or surrender to their sovereignty. At every meal, we decide whether we view the food before us as fuel for our recovery or allow our calorie-counting obsessions to cause further calamity. I keep a little magnet devoted to this choice stuck to my fridge so that I can re-evaluate my restrictive habits every time I approach a meal. "You have the choice to dance," it reads. Thus, when faced with the stress of a sandwich, *I choose* to boogie-woogie with the bologna instead of allowing my anxiety to trigger indigestion. Finally, speaking of faith, every day *we choose* whether or not we have faith in *ourselves* – because it is impossible to claim faith in any distant deity if you don't first find it within your own being.

So, yes, those chaplain visits were something I cherished throughout my hospital stay because they helped me see a purpose beyond my situation. This was awesome because, at that time, my situation kind of sucked! Those visits also helped me overcome the sense of failure I felt for having landed myself in a psychiatric hospital, and instead see my institutionalization as a chance to restore my body, mind and spirit so that I might make the most of the life I had yet to live. Consequently, those visits restored my desire to live!

A lot of good came from those weeks of hospitalization outside of simply getting healthier. I was able to save a good bit of money by crocheting all my Christmas gifts during craft time, I developed a variety of coping skills that continue to get me through clutch times, and I was able to get in more touch with my feminine side as a result of being the only man on a 35-person unit! All said, it was that chaplain's encouragement to seek a purpose larger than myself that truly allowed me to find reason in being there, because when I finally accepted that there was more to live for than food and exercise, I found purpose in taking time to heal. Finally, as I healed, I began to seek out ways to help heal others. For, as it's been said many times and in many ways, you can't help others if you don't help yourself.

With that chaplain's words fresh in mind, I encourage you to ask yourself these three simple-yet-difficult questions:

- Are you willing to help yourself?
- Are you willing to ask for and/or receive help from those who love you?
- How might you utilize your personal journey help others work through their own?

CHAPTER 5.5

A QUICK SUBCHAPTER ON FAITH

"Faith is a marvel that no human being is excluded from. For that in which all human life is united is passion... and faith is passion."

— Soren Kierkegaard

I tend to tiptoe around the topic of faith in a society that discourages any dinner-table dialogue related to politics or religion. However, tiptoe as I may, I am a minister, and this is my book; hence, I feel as though the subject of spirituality has at least earned itself a short sub-chapter. Besides, most everyone reading a book on eating disorders likely dreads dinner tables, so the dialogue that occurs around them is of little concern.

From 40-day fasts to stories of self-deprivation, the topic of disordered eating proved to be quite relevant throughout my graduate studies in theology and philosophy. As a result, I became engulfed in an exploration of the more existential elements of anorexia. From Gandhi to Jesus, and Confucius to Kierkegaard, I was amazed by the prevalence of religious-rooted disordered relationships with food and exercise, and how they were praised and practiced by our past prophets and philosophical forefathers. Furthermore, the deeper that I dove into religion, the more pronounced the disordered roots of time-honored religious rituals proved to be. We fast from food, then we break bread. We abstain from alcohol, then turn water to wine. And for so far as food rules go, the next time you get down on yourself about the rigidity of your own eating, just flip open the Old Testament (the Jewish Torah) and peruse the hundreds of laws that limit the diets of our Hebrew ancestors. Eat this. Sacrifice that. Avoid this. Bless that. Geez! It would seem as though our dietary habits damned us since the start of society.

I heard a pretty good, slightly religious one-liner the other day that might help lighten up the mood if you are ever asked to describe the average anorexic diet. "When asked what it is like to be anorexic," joked a Muslim stand-up comedian, "I've come to compare it to being a vegan Muslim, practicing the Paleo diet during the month of Ramadan."

All jokes aside, thanks in large part to my past enrollment in a slightly exclusionary evangelical institution as an agnostic, anorexic, progressive undergrad, I quickly developed a passion for inclusion that crossed over the chasms formed by differences in faith, economic standing, sexual orientation, gender and/or mental health diagnoses. As a result, I committed to abstain from any religion that:

1. **I cannot laugh at.** (Religion, life and mental health are each far too serious to be taken seriously.)
2. **Prevents me from being "me" while practicing.** (I should not need to put on a fake smile or recite an outdated creed that I don't fully understand to fit in at church.)
3. **I do not view as inclusive TO ALL!** (Individuals of any race, gender, sexual orientation and/or mental health diagnosis must be welcome.)
4. **I see no relevance in.** (Where does this multi-millennia-old tradition fit into my modern-day life?)

With those four self-imposed standards in mind, it was during a Sunday service on one of my self-proclaimed "disorder days" that I first felt truly unwelcome at church. Why? Because my faith in – or fear of – our friend Ed had proven stronger than the awe I felt toward any Biblical fatherly figure. Despite my many attempts to erase that day from my mind, I remember the scene all too vividly. As the sermon came to a close, the ushers had begun to circle the sanctuary with trays of bread and grape juice in hand, in step with the melancholy melody blaring from a 100-year-old organ. "Amen," declared the minister – and my anxiety spiked. I knew what was coming next, and it had been a rough morning, so I knew that I couldn't consume the *calories* of Christ. It was in that instant that I no longer felt welcome in the community that I had sought out for support. I was an outcast – a sinfully skinny anorexic, sitting all alone on a pew amidst a flock of perfect and healthy parishioners.

"The body of Christ, broken for you." The unsuspecting usher, with a loaf of bread in hand, repeated the blessing that he had heard thousands of times throughout his decades of church attendance while staring into my fearful eyes, a loaf of bread in his hand.

Panic! The unassuming usher lowered the loaf before me, and I broke off the smallest chunk of bread that could possibly be broken. What I did next will stick with me for the rest of my life. After what seemed like an hour of deliberation, I raised my shaking hand to my lips and pretended to put the *body of Christ* into my mouth – only to then sneak the small sliver stealthily into my pocket when the usher moved to the next pew. Tears pooled in my eyes as a horrid guilt filled my otherwise empty stomach. I had reached an all-new low.

That little bread mishap turned out to be an influential event in both my personal recovery as well as in my broader spiritual journey. It even inspired me to write an article for a Boston-based journal called *Science and Spirituality*, which you can find footnoted if you'd like to further explore the relationship between eating disorders and religion.[1]

Throughout the course of seminary, my ongoing interest in the arena of spirituality and eating disorders continued to reveal a deep-seated connection between ancient aestheticism and modern-day anorexia. Now that word, aestheticism, might be a foreign term to many, but its meaning is relevant to this story. The word "aesthetic" derives from the Greek *aisthetikos*, which would best be translated as "of sense perception." Thus, throughout the course of

---

1   https://godandnature.asa3.org/opinion-the-breaking-bread.html

human consciousness, religious devotees, or aesthetics, have turned to sensory-stimulating activities, such as fasting, feasting or excessive exercise, to elicit existential encounters with the divine. So, whether this existential, enlightening experience occurs while following in the footsteps of the starving Siddhartha (who became Buddha only after a self-inflicted 49-day fast under a Bodhi tree), praising Allah through the restrictive rules of Ramadan, contemplating Krishna through the practice of intensive yoga, or breaking bread in remembrance of the only begotten son of God, it is undeniable that religious aesthetics have used rituals of self-deprecation and self-expenditure throughout the ages in an effort to communicate with their respective God(s). Christianity's Apostle Paul summed this up by delineating three core "tenets of faith" that he deemed to be essential in authenticating one's spiritual experience. In contemporary Christianity, we refer to these tenets as almsgiving, fasting and prayer; however, in Paul's time, these three practices were known as self-expenditure, self-deprecation and moving outward of oneself.

These three tenets remain relevant to most of the world's religious traditions to this day – in practice, if not in word. Devout Buddhists fast following their noontime meal in hopes of clarifying their thoughts and purifying their body. Pious Jews continue to adhere to the more-than-600 food laws that come with their ritualized calendar of feasts and fasts. Christian mystics have been motivated for millennia to follow in the fasting footsteps of Moses and Jesus, who were each given a divine revelation upon their respective 40-day famines in the desert. And, while modern day anorexic aesthetics don't often journey into the desert, our restrictive eating and compulsive exercise practices have proven to be timeless tactics that people of all faith backgrounds have used to elicit ecstatic experiences and/or control their emotions for eons.

What does this all mean? It means that the roots of eating disorders often go much deeper than suggested by numbers on a scale or images in mirrors. In response, maybe it is time for our society's approach to recovery to move beyond the basics of body restoration and meal planning as well, and touch on some of the spiritual sources of our self-imposed starvation.

CHAPTER 6

RESIDENTIAL AND BEYOND

"Choosing what you do is called freedom; doing what will make you feel free is called happiness."

– Sudha Murty

Now that we've found our way back from that religious rabbit hole, let us pick up where we left off – in that first round of residential treatment. There are any number of reasons why a 19-year-old guy might be resistant to inpatient care – and almost all of them revolve around ego and a perceived loss of freedom. News flash: We surrender our freedom the instant that we first submit to a disordered behavior, and we lose it more every day that we cave into one of those behaviors instead of confronting it head on. Ironically, as I look back, it wasn't until my physical freedom was stripped away by the hospital's take-no-shit staff of nurses that I first felt emotionally free. It was bizarre... but blissful just the same. By not having the choice to behave in a disordered way, I began to realize that I actually did have choices. I began to see that, by clinging to the false perception of physical freedom, I was restricting my ability to live freely, because eating disorders are rooted in self-determined rules that restrict one's freedom. It was during that initial inpatient experience that I first started to figure out that all those self-imposed rules to which I'd been adhering were not actually written in stone. They were not commandments! They were merely suggestions made up by the disorder, which I could amend at any time. Now,

I am aware that many of you lovely readers are not currently in need of residential treatment or not willing to admit that you are, but regardless of where you are on your journey to or through inpatient care, it is essential that we each pause to ask ourselves one simple question: "Am I free?"

If you're at all like me, then your answer – or lack of one – might offer a gentle reminder of why you are reading a book on recovery in the first place. Thus, whereas our definitions of and routes to recovery may differ, our common quest for freedom and our communal call to surrender to recovery will continue to unite us. True, surrender is scary; however, after spending five weeks in the hospital, I was surprised to find that the fear I had of losing my freedom upon entering treatment was actually less than the fear I had of leaving the hospital five weeks later. And why wouldn't it be? After all, the *free* world, with all its choices and voices, can be a super scary place! I relate this back to the existential philosopher Jean-Paul Sartre's depiction of the phenomenon we commonly refer to as vertigo. In this instance, claims Sartre, it is not the fear of falling that throws off our equilibrium, but the fear of knowing that we have a choice to jump.

I still remember what it felt like to walk out of the hospital that fateful first day of restored freedom. I had spent over a month free from decision-making, intensive workouts and the exposure to any external triggers – and now I was scared shitless to face the world I had left behind! I felt vulnerable and fragile, kind of like the feeling one gets when taking the first few steps on a broken foot upon getting a cast removed. For weeks, a bulky plaster shell immobilizes, supports and protects the limp limb within it, allowing the wearer to restore their confidence, while a pair of armpit-chaffing crutches provide balance and support. These casts and crutches free us from the fear of further fracture so that we can focus our energy on recovery. Much the same, inpatient care provides a cast to protect us from Ed's sadistic suggestions and the dangers of the real world around us. By surrendering to residential treatment, we gain the support and supervision of a team of specialists who work with us in addressing our nutritional, emotional and psychiatric needs. Having a trusted team around us allows us to stop overthinking recovery so that we can actually start recovering; however, this requires that we trust them! All that said, for as safe a space as a hospital may be, if it is freedom that you seek, then you cannot stay hidden inside that cast forever. Thus, there comes a time when we must break free and face the real world... and, for me, that time had come.

It was my first evening of independence. My mom had reserved a room for me in a hotel adjacent to the hospital so that I could check into the day program bright and early the next morning. However, for the moment, I was free – alone and unsupervised with only one thing on my plate. Literally! I had to prepare and eat evening snack on my own. Now, that sounds easy enough, but five sedentary weeks in a psych unit had left me stiff and sore. I yearned for a good walk. My metaphorical cast had been removed, and there were miles upon miles of open sidewalk before me. Still, I was scared to put strain on my broken body again. I remembered running mile after mile just over a month before, but now that I was free to move again, I feared even a slow stroll – my mind was racing.

What if I can't stop? What if I can't start? What will it feel like to move? What is too much? What is too little? What is normal and what is disordered? What will I tell my therapist tomorrow if the metal arm of the scale leans to the lighter side? What will I tell myself if it tilts to the heavy side? What will I have for snack tonight? Can I eat it alone? Can I stop eating once I start? Am I hungry? Am I full? AHHHHH!

So much for a relaxing starlit stroll... I wanted my inpatient cast back!

My fears slowly subsided in the days and weeks to come as I continued to test my strength and flex my freedom, though I can't claim the process was particularly pleasant. True, there was an aspect of adventure interwoven with my hesitancy as I continued to explore the life I'd left behind, but I couldn't quite free myself from the fear that I would push – or be pushed – too far.

"Wow! You look so much healthier, Ryan!" a neighbor exclaimed as I shut my mailbox.

Healthier? I cringed. *What does that mean?* "Thank you," I mumbled in reply.

Later that evening, a family friend dropped by to say hello and said, "It's so great to see you with a little padding back on your bones!"

OUCH! That one hurt. I forced myself to smile, all the while wishing they'd turn around and wander back out the door. *Why did they have to use that word… padding?*

"You're back!" My friends cheered when we met up for the first time. "And looking so much better!"

For most people, "better" would be a blessing, but in the mind of an anorexic, "better" simply meant "bigger." And bigger was uncomfortable! I was uncomfortable! My body felt bloated, my interactions felt awkward, and my sanity felt strained.

That awkwardness continued for several weeks, and as much as I hate to admit it, I've realized that discomfort is simply something you are going to have expect after a stint of residential treatment. The world doesn't always know how to act or what to say upon our re-entry into it. It felt as though there was no right response from friends or family those first few weeks back in the real world – and as much as I wanted to be gracious to them, I secretly yearned for everyone to just shut up.

Though those first days felt more like years, my confidence slowly started to creep up and, before long, I began to brush off triggering conversations. Or maybe I should say that I stopped being triggered by every conversation! I owe much of this to a simple visualization exercise led by my therapist, which helped me see my hospitalization as a cocoon instead of a cast – a slight, albeit significant shift from brokenness to beauty.

Visualization can be an amazing tool, and it has been an essential part of my personal recovery over the years. With that in mind, what do you say we walk through the kind of corny meditation that has granted me confidence and comfort throughout the past two decades? You're not the meditation type, you say? Not true… like anything else worthwhile in this life, it just requires a little practice. So, suck it up, get comfortable, and give it a go.

Take a deep breath in while acknowledging each of your present emotions – pleasant or unpleasant as they may be. Hold that breath for a few seconds. Accept those feelings instead of fleeing from them.

Now exhale. As you do, allow the triggers, traumas and to-dos of your day to drift away into the great abyss along with your breath. Allow yourself to simply be present in the moment.

Breathe in, remaining attentive to the unique sounds and smells of your surroundings.

Then, exhale away any fears of the future or pains from the past.

Repeat this pattern several more times until you find a place of peace and presence.

Now, envision yourself as a caterpillar, tucked cozily inside a dangling cocoon. You are safe and secure, protected by a nature-sewn shell while swaying back and forth in the breeze.

Feel the movement of the outside world. Feel your wings as they form at your sides. Clench each of your muscles, from your toes to your nose, and explore the strength of your own body as it presses against the hard shell that surrounds you. Relax. You're strong, graceful and beautiful.

As you hang there, swaying back and forth in the breeze, you begin to dream of a destiny much larger than the cocoon that encapsulates you.

Take another deep breath in, this time stretching your arms outward. When you exhale, push hard against the walls that surround you until you feel the shell shatter and fall to the ground below. You are free! And as you extend your arms for the first time, you feel something new: WINGS! You have wings! Now it is time to spread them and fly.

This is the freedom we must claim when the fears of recovery tempt us to restrict, relapse or become reclusive. True, there will be times that we feel broken, as well as times that we need a cast and crutches to hobble our way along recovery road. But we are not broken. We are butterflies, called forth to break free from our cocoons, spread our wings and reclaim our beauty.

That imagery is enchanting and exciting, but beware: This metamorphosis is not easy, and true transformation always requires surrender. Before we spread our wings, we must first commit to the cocoon. What does that mean in your life? What is the cocoon to which you are called, and where do you want to fly when you break free from it? Maybe you are currently trudging through a difficult stage of treatment and you're ready to test out your newfound strengths. If so, what is preventing you from spreading your wings and soaring? Maybe you are coming to terms with your inner caterpillar, and you're just now inching toward treatment. If so, what is standing in your way? No matter what stage of recovery you are in, two questions will always be relevant: Do you want to be free? And are you able to accept that you are beautiful?

CHAPTER 7

WHY IS ED YELLING SO LOUDLY?

Recovery can – and hopefully will – feel freeing, but it is far from all bliss and butterflies. In reality, recovery can be a bitch. Thus, I'd like to acknowledge a rather agonizing question that many of us face upon breaking free from our cocoons: Why is the voice of my eating disorder speaking so much louder now that I am attempting recovery than it was when I was living disordered?

That question seems simple at first glimpse, so let us start with a simple answer: The volume knob on our buddy Ed gets cranked up because, upon confronting our adversary, we also acknowledge its existence. In other words, by resisting Ed, we also give him our full attention – and now that we are in dialogue with that damn disorder, it is impossible to return to ignorance, no matter how badly we may want to!

Simple as that answer may sound, simplicity can still be complicated for the malnourished mind to comprehend. So, let us muse over this one together with the help of a metaphor – one of my most-loved literary tricks.

I live in Santa Cruz, California, land of beautiful beaches and really cold water. Living with an eating disorder is somewhat like lying on the hot sand with the sun scorching your skin from above. Go there for a moment. Picture yourself on a pristine beach, peering out over a beautiful blue ocean. The sun is shining on your shoulders while a swarm of seagulls soar and squawk overhead. At first, the heat feels good, but as time ticks by, the sun starts to get a little too intense. Things begin to get uncomfortable.

The water sure does look refreshing – tempting, to say the least. But you have become accustomed to the heat, and you always stay on the sand, so you sit in submission while the sun continues to sear your skin. True, it may be a little uncomfortable, but the sand is safe. So, what do you do? Perhaps you slather on some sunscreen and scan the shoreline to find a little shade. Still, the cool ocean continues to call out to you. But the ocean is unknown and intimidating, and there is a too much effort involved in getting up off your beach blanket to test its waters. Instead, you choose to sit in the sun and succumb to its burn. Why? Because, regardless of the unpleasantries of a sandy sunburn, it is at least familiar.

We call this complacency, and while many people accept it as a lifestyle, we must remember that, much like skin cancer, complacency can kill – literally! As the National Institute on Health asserts, eating disorders are the deadliest of all mental illnesses.[2] However, this complacency is figuratively fatal as well, because living with an eating disorder is not truly living. Thus, though many commit to a slightly sunburnt lifestyle on the metaphorical shoreline, there are some for whom the refreshing ocean of recovery speaks louder than the anxieties that keep us dry. By making it through the first several chapters of this book, you have admitted that you are at least considering being one of those brave souls who wishes to wade into the waves of wellness. You have admitted that you are not satisfied with your current situation in the sand, despite the uncertainties that will arise upon entering the ocean.

I often relate the early stages of recovery to those first few steps into icy water. After we make the decision to go for a swim, we can't return to the sand we've left behind because it's too hot; however, the ocean that calls out to us is too cold to be comfortable. The result? We find ourselves stuck in a painfully soggy purgatory, waist-deep in waiting while our ridiculous eating disorder anxieties continue to

---

2   https://www.nimh.nih.gov/health/publications/eating-disorders

intensify because we made the decision to address them. Fortunately – though it can feel unfortunate in the moment – the initial bliss that greets us upon taking those first steps into the waters of recovery keeps us from ever again being content with our situation on the shore. We know that we cannot live a life of anorexic ignorance, but we are uncertain as to whether we have what it takes to fully surrender to the sea of recovery.

I've said it several times thus far, and I will say it again: If I have learned one thing on my journey, it is that transformation requires surrender. That may sound extreme to someone whose illness is based on the need to claim control of every aspect of life, but given that you are reading a book on recovery, you likely have subconsciously surrendered control of your life to the disorder a long time ago. So, why not take a dive into the unknown? Why not surrender yourself to recovery instead of restriction? Why not wade into those waves of wellness instead of wasting your days living disordered, distant and distracted?

An eating disorder of any type loves to feed – yet another ironic truth – on learned behaviors. When faced with events or emotions outside of our control, Ed likes to taunt us with compulsory responses, such as skipping a meal, sneaking in an extra workout, or binging and purging. Those responses, as unhealthy as they may be, temporarily lessen our anxiety by giving us back control and familiarity – or, at least, giving us the perception that we have them. These behaviors seem safe in the short term, but like any drug, they elicit an experience of physical or emotional release on which we become dependent. Thus, every time that we give in to a disordered behavior to alleviate our anxiety in the present, we allow the disorder to strengthen its future hold on us. Surrendering to these learned behaviors and responses gives them power.

Returning to our metaphorical ocean, succumbing to an eating disorder behavior is like trying to reduce the splash of an incoming wave by turning away from it instead of diving headfirst through it. This metaphor illustrates why recovery is so intense. Upon stepping into the sea, all the disordered behaviors that once eased our past anxieties now cause anxiety. Why? Because we know they no longer serve us, and we cannot play ignorant to their negative effects. We know that we need to confront our compulsions, but we don't feel strong enough to do so. Thus, we turn our backs to the waves and get walloped by them instead of gliding gracefully through them. We put off the discomforts of recovery until tomorrow and submit ourselves to the pounding of the disorder today. We know that we need to dive fully into the ocean if we ever hope to be free, but the thought of the cold water keeps us stranded in that aforementioned purgatory, a painful middle ground where acting on unhealthy behaviors increases our anxiety, but making healthy choices is too intense to offer up an easy alternative. As a result, we are left in the middle of an argument between two voices every time we face a decision: the voice of our eating disorder, which taunts us with familiarity; and the voice of logic, which, in the moment, seems so illogical.

My first few months of recovery were exhausting because the inner argumentativeness of my authentic voice, coupled with the voice of the disorder, became too loud to let in any other voices. This dueling dialogue left me unable to think about anything other than my disorder or be present in any activity that might offer a momentary distraction from my disease. I spent many a night lying in bed, dreading awakening to another day, and I feared free time, because having free time meant I would have to make decisions on how to utilize it, and with decision-making came my anxiety-evoking nemesis: indecisiveness. Thus, my fears of surrendering to recovery have repeatedly pushed me toward the less-pleasant purgatorial approach – and I've only wound up more beaten down because of it.

Don't get discouraged, though, because with each uncomfortable choice we make, Ed's voice gets a teeny-weeny bit quieter. (Note that no one ever said this was going to be a quick fix!) Take heart because, in time, that evil eating disorder dialogue WILL dissipate, even if only one *teeny-weeny bit* at a time. As it does, the healthier voices of your therapists and friends, the wind in the trees, the laughter of little children and your authentic self will continue to get more pronounced. You will start to hear the world around you over the voice of that obnoxious eating disorder within. It isn't that our healthy, logical voice overtakes Ed's annoyingly unreasonable one, nor that choosing recovery will eliminate all our anxieties. It's that each time we choose to focus on the voice of recovery instead of submitting to the suggestions of our disorder, we reinforce the reality that we are not our eating disorders. YOU ARE NOT YOUR EATING DISORDER!

CHAPTER 8

LEARNING HOW TO FLY: FINDING ORDER IN A DISORDERED WORLD

I worked hard to shift my mindset from anxiety to excitement ahead of the spring semester of my sophomore year, and when it was finally time to drive back to Tennessee, I honestly thought I was ready to spread my wings. Unfortunately, although I was ready for Tennessee, it just so happened that Tennessee wasn't quite ready for me! I quickly came to find that there was very little support in the arena of eating disorder recovery available in that small Smoky Mountain town. Though it took some searching, I did eventually find a counselor, and with her help, I then formed an accountability team, comprised of a few trustworthy friends and two of our school's athletic trainers, to keep me honest and eating. The process was not easy – and it is important to remember that even our best friends are far from therapists.

This deficiency in care is common in many small towns and rural areas around the world. And even in cities where resources are readily available, we still must overcome many obstacles to get help. In fact, through my experience as both a patient and provider, I've come to the sad conclusion that the painstaking process of finding adequate mental health care is far too often a cause of mental breakdown! Take that as a foreshadowing of my inevitable relapse if you wish, but for now, let me simply state that the goal of this writing is not to fix the system, but to empower those of us who are stuck navigating it with a starved psyche. On reflection, I now see that the lack of accessible care that I experienced while in Tennessee did come with a silver lining. Being forced into a do-it-yourself treatment model made me take an active role in assessing my situation, discerning my weaknesses and getting strategic about where I needed support. In other words, not having a perfectly paved path forced me to be proactive in my recovery.

One defect of the more prescriptive paths of treatment lies in the one-size-fits-all style of treatment that these institutions use to address eating disorders and addictions. This type of plan makes it incredibly easy for participants to pass off any responsibility for their own recovery while parading along a preordained path. True, the six-meals-a-day, cookie-cutter model of treatment would be great if we were all similarly disordered (or if we were able to talk about cookies without cringing); however, every eating disorder is different. Thus, as a slightly atypical patient myself, I've never fit well into traditional treatment plans.

What does this all mean? It means that, regardless of how well you've mapped out your path, there is no way around the simple truth that recovery requires hard work – and that it will always remain a work in progress.

In the months following my return to Tennessee, I was able to find a bit of balance, but a strange thing had occurred during my time in residential care. Somehow, over the course of those five weeks, I had shifted from restriction to addiction. So, whereas before treatment I would anxiously avoid eating, I now had trouble stopping! True, it was fantastic that I was eating again, but at some point during my hospitalization, I developed an incessant and rather isolating obsession over when I was eating, what I was eating and with whom I was eating – not to mention that I had also developed the appetite of one of those hotdog-eating-contest champions!

So, what did I do? I decided to use my obsessive-compulsive kookiness (a notably kinder word than "craziness") as a crutch to help me navigate my recovery pathway. That shift in wording, from "crazy" to "kooky", was actually an important step in my quest for self-acceptance. Accepting our craziness as kookiness allows us to be a bit more playful when dealing with Ed and all his absurdities. Whereas the *crazy* Ryan felt he had to hide his abnormal mealtime behaviors, the *kooky* Ryan was able to laugh at the many idiosyncrasies he'd adopted during treatment and use his obsessiveness to his advantage.

Re-creating the regimented lifestyle of the hospital wasn't too difficult in a college setting since my day was broken down into convenient little hour-long blocks that divided class time, mealtime, practice and study; however, it proved to be a little more difficult in the real world some years later. We'll eventually dive deeper into those real-world struggles I faced, but for now, let's just say that, in the 20-some years that I have researched eating disorders and addiction, I have yet to find anyone whose recovery thrives on *dis*order. No, structure and accountability are essential in overcoming a disorder rooted in, well, a lack of order. For me that meant finding balance between restriction and addiction, healthy activity and over-exercise, and interaction and isolation.

Did "balance" mean that I didn't experience anxiety? Absolutely not! But I started to learn ways to address it that didn't involve excessive exercise or an Ativan pill.

Did I distance myself from ol' Ed enough that his voice disappeared? Not a chance! There were days when the disorder didn't just speak, it shouted. I have had to accept that these days – while they may not be avoidable, enjoyable or productive – do indeed pass.

Was I normal? Ha! What is normal? We are all kooky! Some of us just happen to be a little kookier about certain things than others.

So, what did a balanced life look like? It started off with eliminating exercise. This was not easy, and it left me with a lot of unstructured time throughout my day, which I used my creativity to fill. I would plan little field trips, seek out social activities and experiment with new hobbies, all in an attempt distract myself from any disordered thoughts that arose. Anything that I could do to add an element of enjoyment to my otherwise anxious life was fair game. (Note the language I used there: enjoyment. Though it may not be easy, with proper intention, a little practice and possibly the help of a prescription or two, pleasure is possible in recovery. After all, most of the world would dance with joy at the thought of forced laziness and lavish lunch spreads!)

I remember working alongside the college administration that spring in order to get a key to the school's art studio. That way, I could continue cultivating the newfound passion for painting that I had picked up during my time in the hospital. I also worked with a nutritionist in town to create a list of diverse food options that I could mix and match to craft a three-meal-a-day diet. Together, we drew up a structured meal plan that also included a wildcard nighttime snack, with which I was encouraged to get a little wacky. I met weekly with a therapist who helped me distinguish between disordered and logical thoughts, and together we brainstormed how to best challenge the former with the latter. All in all, I spent the spring semester tiptoeing my way along recovery road while restoring my mind, body and spirit.

As time passed by and my weight stabilized, I began to feel as though I was truly finding my footing in recovery. Not long thereafter, I also regained the confidence and energy necessary to use that newly found footing, quite literally, to reclaim my passion for running. This could be seen as a red flag to many in the recovery world, but before it became tied to restricting, running had been an aspect of my identity that brought me much pleasure – that is, when I wasn't using it as a means of self-punishment! Upon getting healthy, I was no longer willing to surrender that passion to some stupid disorder; so, I formed an accountability team – consisting of my coach, the school's athletic training staff and my therapist – who would walk with me as I slowly re-entered the sport. And re-entry started off with just that... walking! After two weeks of walking and weight gain, under the watchful eyes of the athletic training team, my request to add a short jog to the tail end of my walk every other day was granted. Along with that expanded workout, a strange and foreign feeling from my past also crept back into my life: strength. I felt strong! I had beaten myself down for years via restriction and overexertion, and as a result, I had grown accustomed to feeling completely and chronically exhausted. As unpleasant as this exhaustion may have been, I secretly craved it because it felt safe. It numbed my emotions and helped alleviate my guilt – temporarily, at least. But this new, more vibrant, version of me... it felt good! I liked feeling strong! I liked it, and I didn't want to lose it. After years of starvation had stripped my speed from me, it was euphoric to feel fast, and I cannot begin to explain the elation that came with identifying as an athlete instead of an anorexic.

Was my return to running the most recovery-minded move? That's up for debate. However, it was essential in allowing me to reclaim my identity and confidence. Furthermore, as I continued to gain physical strength, I also developed the emotional and cognitive resilience necessary to challenge my disordered thinking. So, in opposition to my pre-residential, run-down running mentality, I began to view running as a means of pursuing recovery instead of fleeing from it. Furthermore, with the help of my nutritionist, I started to incorporate healthy meals and rest into my training plan – a process that also required me to do something that, mere months before, would have sounded utterly absurd: to eat on rest days. (What a novel concept that was – suppers independent of sweat.) It was also during this time that I began to distinguish between mindful (enjoyable) and mindless (anxiety-based) movement. This allowed me to view exercise as an element of a much larger life, although that also meant that I had to figure out what life beyond exercise and athletics was all about, not to mention what I would do with all that newfound free time.

My pursuit of purpose beyond exercise eventually led me to one very special person named Darrell. I met Darrell through Best Buddies, a nationwide nonprofit that matches college-aged students with individuals living with disabilities. In all honesty, my initial involvement with the program was a little less altruistic than you might think. The truth was, I had a crush on the founder of our college's Best Buddies chapter, and I figured that my chances of buddying up with that blond beauty might be better if I joined her club. To my credit, I did end up dating her; however, the more fulfilling and lasting relationship was the one I formed with my buddy Darrell.

Darrell taught me more than any college professor or therapist could during my undergraduate years in Tennessee. He would greet me bright and early in morning with a glow on his face, a hunger in his belly and an outpouring of excitement for the day ahead. Darrell's outlook on life mirrored the simple-yet-profound wisdom of the stuffed animal that joined us on all our outings, A.A. Milne's whimsical Winnie-the-Pooh.

> *"When you wake up in the morning, Pooh," Piglet said at last, "what's the first thing you say to yourself?"*
> *"What's for breakfast?" said Pooh. "What do you say, Piglet?"*
> *"I say, 'I wonder what's going to happen exciting today?'"*
> *Pooh nodded thoughtfully. "It's the same thing," he said.*

If I had to explain the effect of my disorder on my soul these past two decades, I would say it *Pooh-ed* all over my spirit of excitement and left me with the nervous energy of his Piglet friend. *What is going to happen to me today? What voice do I trust? What if I can't work out? What if I have to eat something scary?* Working with Darrell taught me how to stop fearing things such as breakfast, and how to get excited about the opportunities that these seemingly scary things held in making each day more beautiful. Darrell taught me how to embrace the moment.

Darrell didn't dramatize dessert; he dreamed about it. He didn't overanalyze every situation; he simply lived life. Darrell didn't feel the need to change who he was; he enjoyed being himself. So, while I wrestled with an incredibly complex disorder, the simple wisdom of my Winnie-the-Pooh-loving partner made all the difference in the world. To this day, I continue to work with a community of amazing individuals who are far too often defined by their perceived lack of ability, and I encourage you to volunteer your time and open your heart in a similar way. Why? Because the unadulterated acceptance and love that these exceptional human beings have to offer can teach all of us how to better love and accept ourselves.

The remaining three years of college flew by, and I graduated in the winter of 2006 with bachelor's degrees in both theology and English, as well as with plans to enroll in graduate school that fall. Needless to say, upon receiving my diploma, I thought I could use a little reprieve following an overall enjoyable, but undoubtably exhausting four-year fight with early-morning exams, English essays and a disordered friend named Ed. So, before diving back into the world of academia, I took a semester off to further pursue my inner Pooh, this time serving as an afterschool daycare leader for a bunch of elementary schoolers. To my delight, much like working with the special needs community, I found that interacting with children provided a constant reminder of how to be playful, grateful and present. And I'll be damned if those little Pooh bears didn't even teach me how to look forward to something as intimidating, as scary, as… SCRUMPTIOUS as snack time! Yes, Fruit Roll-Ups and juice boxes beware, those little elementary-school-aged psychologists got me to snack alongside them between kickball and coloring every afternoon. How did they do it? By making playfulness my prescription for panic.

Academia and afterschool care aside, upon graduation, my running career also advanced beyond the collegiate cross-country level, and I soon worked my way onto the semi-professional marathon circuit. Now, I cannot claim that the adherence to a marathon training plan helped with my rigidity, but it did at least keep me honest about my weight, rest and eating habits. As I've alluded, there are multiple definitions that we could toss around in terms of recovery, but in this instance, two types of individuals in recovery stand out to me. The first are those who distance themselves from Ed to the point that they can claim complete freedom from the scale, calorie counting and all those debilitating disordered behaviors. I can't describe what this breed of recovery feels like because I have admittedly never experienced it. On the other side of the recovery rainbow, there are those like yours truly, who reach a point where they look healthy, maintain a balanced diet and live a generally enjoyable and successful life, but remain in dialogue with a dormant-yet-still-very-present disorder. I spent a lot of afternoons interviewing many of my peers while writing this book, and what I came to find is that many of these more intense, mostly type-A individuals are often able to thrive in the world if − and that is a big "if" − they are able to figure out a healthy life balance in which their ED-derived discipline keeps them motivated and moving forward.

Throughout my latter years of college and into post-graduate life, I was one of these people. I learned how to keep Ed at a safe distance – never so close as to corrupt my recovery, but never so far out of sight to surrender my perceived control and truly recover. I would never allow my weight to drop below my doctor's stated "unhealthy" level, but I'd also never allow it to rise above a self-set limit, either. I would never skip a meal, but I was never able to enjoy one fully and freely. It was a delicate dance, and it worked well for several years... but I soon came to find out that *delicate* can be pretty damn dangerous!

CHAPTER 9

FROM DELICATE TO DOWNFALL

I had sprung into the spring that year with a hop in my step – so much hop, in fact, that I placed second in the inaugural Under Armor Marathon in Baltimore a mere three days after receiving an acceptance letter from Louisville Seminary, along with word that I had been awarded a full academic scholarship for graduate school. I was invincible! I felt blessed and balanced, and at the ripe old age of 23, as though I had life all figured out. I would join the professional marathon circuit and make a run at the Olympic trials while pursuing a master's degree in divinity, then begin a ministerial career through which I would help the world reimagine religion, thanks to my progressive perspective on faith. Yep, I was happy, healthy, hopeful and, at the time, only a little bit hindered by my disorder. But damn, what a difference a day makes.

"I'll secure his neck. You work on the bleeding." Though my memory of that fateful afternoon might be a bit foggy, I'll never forget the muddled voices of those first responders. My life had changed in an instant, and I was nothing but a helpless observer to my own demise.

"You doing alright, buddy?"

"Huh? Yeah," I mumbled. "I think so…" However, the blood that poured out from my mouth as I spoke made me second guess my answer. I had recently taken up cycling as a means of avoiding running injuries, and yet there I was, laying limp on the ground in a pool of my own blood after going for a relaxing recovery ride one Sunday afternoon. Irony is a bitch.

"Just stay still and bite on this," the EMT said as he shoved a roll of gauze into my mouth. I closed my eyes and listened to the nightmare unfold around me.

"Code nine... repeat, code nine! We are bringing in a young adult male victim of a pedestrian-vehicular collision with a possible neck fracture and head trauma."

Fractured neck!? I wiggled my toes while drifting in and out of consciousness to see if I could still feel them within my shoes. I had just been T-boned by a minivan whose driver had texted his way through a red light at 40mph.

"Up you go!" The stretcher they had strapped me into bumped and clunked as they slid me into the ambulance. "We'll be at the hospital in no time. Just keep biting on that gauze and try to stay awake."

To this day, that trip to the trauma center remains nothing but a blur of sirens, sharp turns and a three-way phone conversation between the EMT, my mother and myself.

"Yes, ma'am, he seems coherent despite some head and neck trauma." The medic attempted to pacify my mother; however, I could hear the panic that filled her voice as she spoke to him.

"Yes, ma'am, he is able to speak." The EMT slowly lowered the receiver to my ear.

"I am okay, Mom." I knew that I would need to say something a little more convincing if I hoped to calm her down after the medic's abrupt call. "Unfortunately, my bike was not so lucky. I think I might need a new one for my birthday this fall." I hoped a little humor would keep her from hopping on an airplane to Kentucky because I knew that I was about to enter a dark place, and I didn't want to bring anyone down with me.

For the most part, I was able to recover from the accident in the months to follow – physically, that is. But I never healed enough to proceed with my life plans or continue playing off my athletic-derived ego as some sort of self-acceptance. I knew that I was going to need to reassess my life, my disorder and my purpose in the coming months; however, I also knew that I had failed to build a solid enough foundation in my recovery from which to do so. There is a popular Biblical allegory that transcends any one faith tradition and strikes me as particularly relevant in recovery. It forewarns us not to build our lives on shifting sand, and that accident made it quite apparent that I had built my post-treatment life upon the same unsteady ground that had landed me in treatment in the first place. Now – bed-bound, bloody and bruised – I felt as though I was starting from scratch. The only problem was that this time around, I was attempting it without the support and structure of the inpatient unit of my past.

***

Alright… you've been passively participating in my story for plenty of pages now, so what do you say we take a break for a little experiment? It's just a quick exercise to help us all grow an awareness of the shifting sands on which we stand – not to mention, a refreshing reprieve for any of you that might be drifting into dreamland!

Early on I mentioned that I am an aspiring yogi, and as such, my favorite pose has always been the tree. Tree pose is the one in which the yogi stands tall on a single foot while placing the sole of the other foot on the calf or thigh of the supporting leg. When the wind is not blowing, the ground is not sandy, our gaze is not wandering, and the sounds of the world around us flow in rhythm with our thoughts, it is not too difficult to find balance. However, when any one of those conditions is less than ideal, the tree pose can be a colossal challenge.

I was able to find some semblance of balance in the years following my first round of residential treatment by building a life upon the foundation of a superficial athletic career and a little academic success. I had figured out just how much, and of what, I needed to eat to support my level of activity. I could clear my head with a good run when the adversities of everyday life caused me anxiety. My self-confidence was high because I had hope for the future – and for the most part, I felt firm-footed and balanced. Then, suddenly, the sands below me shifted, and I was left wavering and wobbling in the wind. And I fell.

Experiment time! What do you say we do a little test to see how balanced you are today?

Put down your book or e-reader and stand up. Without any thought or preparation, cast your gaze off into the distance and place the sole of your right foot on the calf or thigh of your left. Some of you may feel balanced enough on this day and at this time to pull off the pose. More often than not, however, our lack of intention and concentration will leave us flailing.

Okay, if you haven't yet fallen from your tree, you have permission to set your foot back down on solid ground. Great job! Now, let's try it once more. This time, before attempting to balance on one foot, kick off your shoes, close your eyes and take a few deep breaths. Pause to feel the ground beneath both feet before lifting either. Is the earth underneath you flat or irregular? Is it cold or warm? Is it natural or human-made? Allow yourself to be present in the moment and put your focus on building an awareness of your surroundings and emotions.

Envision yourself as a tree – strong and stable. Feel your roots as they extend downward from your feet and deep into the earth below. You are balanced and supported. You are strong and stable. Stay here for a moment and simply enjoy the feeling of being rooted.

Now, open your eyes. Fix your stare upon a steady point on the ground in front of you – something steadfast and firm. Take a few breaths here; then, when you feel relaxed and ready, raise your left foot up to the inner calf or thigh of the right leg. How do you feel?

As we return from this brief meditative break, take a moment to think about the foundation and intentionality of your personal recovery journey, then ask yourself:

- **Is my recovery conditional?** (i.e., I can have a snack *if* I get in a walk; I can take a rest day *if* I work out tomorrow; I can eat a cookie *because* it is my birthday; I will recover *for* my mom, spouse, etc.)

- **Is my ability to achieve balance based on external aspects of life or my own rootedness?** If it is the former, then what happens when the world doesn't go your way? If it is the latter, then from what source is that intrinsic desire to heal derived?
- **Is your hopefulness for the future dependent on career, physical or relational achievements?** If so, how will you respond when your expectations go awry and you get T-boned by a speeding minivan!?
- **Are you recovering for someone else or for yourself?** Maybe I should ask: Are you – the authentic you that existed before the world told you who to be – worthy of recovery? Are you worthy of joy? Finally, are you willing to work to achieve that joy?

I was incredibly lucky to find my footing in the years following my first round of inpatient treatment, despite some not-so-recovery-minded answers to those questions above. Thus, for a few years, I stayed pretty balanced. Unfortunately, when your recovery is built upon an uncertain and ego-derived athletic career, it is only a matter of time before something happens to knock you off balance. In my case, that something just so happened to be a Chrysler minivan!

Following that fateful accident, I began to do that simple tree exercise upon waking up every morning – once I was able to stand, that is – and to this day, I'm still amazed by how a little intentionality can push my day in a much more desirable direction. Some mornings, upon raising my foot, I feel rested and ready for the day. On those days, I find that I can stand steady on my first attempt. However, there are many mornings on which I waiver. Those days require a little more work! We all know these days well. They are the ones in which we hit every red light on the way to work, spill coffee on our laps and get ambushed by all the absurd anxieties of our disorders along the way. But have heart, because by pausing amidst our peril and re-rooting ourselves in recovery, we begin to realize that we possess the power to shift our energy and reclaim our inner-tree-ness. It just requires a little extra intentionality on occasion. Now, back to the story.

***

It was while lying in bed those long days following my accident that I realized something very scary: My recovery was a lie. I couldn't eat knowing that I couldn't burn off the calories by running. My anxiety quickly spiraled out of control without being able to exercise it off, and I couldn't clear my mind enough to read or write, which meant I risked losing my academic scholarship – along with my sanity – every day that I dove deeper into bed-ridden depression. So, there I lied, assessing the lie that was my life, while my faith, friendships and fun-loving persona faded away and left me feeling like a fraud.

Fraudulence has been a prominent feeling throughout my life, and I suspect that I am not alone in that. The "me" that the world sees has always felt like a far-flung version of the me that dwells in the depressive or disordered depths of my soul. When that accident stripped me of my athletic identity, I was left with only my shortcomings to show. This kicked off a depressive cycle that lasted nearly a year, and though its intensity wavered day to day, it wasn't until I met a man by the name of Jack that I truly started to see a light.

"Want to go to church with me next Sunday?" Jack asked one day. This was strange question for a variety of reasons:

1. **First,** in a society that dodges conversations about politics and religion, not many people talk about church anymore, let alone share invitations to go to one.
2. **Secondly,** we were standing in a church sanctuary on a Sunday morning when the invitation arose. I was teaching a Sunday school class as part of a seminary internship at the time, and Jack, along with his two daughters, were a few of my weekly regulars. So, I already went to church, and he knew I'd be there next week, too.
3. **Finally,** Jack was undoing his belt as he spoke!

"Um, sure," I answered while trying not to look down as he dropped his trousers. "But we already go to church together every Sunday, Jack."

"No, we sit in a church every Sunday." He said with a smile as he stepped out from his slacks, only to reveal the sleek black cycling spandex that had been hiding underneath them. "Church is what happens afterwards."

I hadn't known Jack for more than a few months at the time, and though the Sunday school class I led at the church was meant for middle-schoolers, this middle-aged man had become my favorite student. I would have discouraged any other parent from attending, but Jack was special. Despite his age – and a stage-four cancer diagnosis – he exuded the most youthful energy of any student in the group. Every Sunday morning, Jack would show up with a Starbucks cup in one hand, a Bible in the other, and a smile stretched from cheek to cheek. Then, as I came to find, every Sunday afternoon he would strip down to his spandex to *attend church* via his trusty, steel-framed Bianca bicycle.

"So… what do you say? Are you up for getting back on a bike next week and joining me for church?" Jack knew all about my accident – those scars were hard to hide. However, he knew nothing about my disorder, the truly debilitating disease that kept me dancing with depression. Had the invitation come from anyone other than Jack, I probably would have turned it down, but knowing what this man was battling, I decided to disregard my fear of both bike and disorder and accept his offer.

Fast-forward a week, and it was a gorgeous Sunday – 70 degrees with a few puffy clouds breaking up a clear blue sky. But just as the two of us were set to embark on a slow cycling church service, a strong headwind started to swirl. I cringed. Throughout my life, I've found that my anxiety likes to spiral out of control whenever I'm exposed to loud sounds, shifts of temperature or, as proven on this day, strong winds. This oversensitivity to the elements of an unpredictable world leaves me susceptible to a panic attack at any given moment – a vulnerability that only worsens when I am underweight or stressed. Unfortunately, I was both at the time, so I felt my chest tighten with the swaying of the trees above. But Jack? He just smiled.

"Do you feel that?"

"Yeah," I said, trying to mask my mounting stress. "We probably want to take another route. Something a little more sheltered?"

That is how I've always treated my disorder. I dodge any face-to-face – or wind-in-the-face – confrontations with Ed by taking all the detours along the way. However, the dying man whose pedals spun next to mine shared a different perspective on the situation. He wanted to face it head on.

"The wind..." Jack paused momentarily in appreciation of the breeze now blowing across his face. "That's God gifting us a free hill workout – without us even needing to find a hill!" His right cheek tightened into a smile. "What a great an opportunity to grow a little stronger!" On a quick aside, I assure you that there are actually plenty of hills in Louisville, so "finding one" was not of my deepest concern; however, Jack's spirit was infectious, nonetheless.

Jack passed away several months after that bike ride, but not before we were able to share many miles and stories. I'll always remember sitting in Hebrew class just after Jack's death. "*Ruach*," the instructor whispered, in a way that made his voice sound like the breeze. "It means wind." He paused. "However, the literal translation is quite larger than that. *Ruach*, in Hebrew, is better defined as 'breath of God.'"

Indeed, it is, I thought as I daydreamed of that day alongside my cycling sage. I still hate the feeling of a strong wind on my face, but I've never approached life's headwinds in the same way. That linguistic lesson, along with Jack's silver-lined perspective on the challenges of life, squelched any self-pity I previously felt.

Why me? Why did I get hit by a car? Why did I become anorexic? I'd often whine to the universe during the dark days leading up to the one on which I first rode with Jack. However, his approach to adversity forced me to rethink my resentments and welcome a spirit of inquiry instead. Before meeting Jack, I would hide behind self-victimization, but his positive outlook on life helped me transform my self-pity into purpose. Thus, instead of whining, "Why me?" every time the world whipped me on the ass, I started asking, "I *wonder* why me?" It was a slight-yet-significant difference that embodied the spirit of my cancer-stricken cycling buddy.

Jack's spirit of wonder challenged me to close a chapter of my personal story, much like I am winding up the one that you are reading today. But before we dive into the next one, how about we each take a second to stop and wonder for ourselves. Wonder why we have been given this opportunity to grow. Wonder what we are called to learn from it. And finally, wonder how we might share the wisdom that we have gained through our experiences with the world.

Why? Because the best means of overcoming the pains and perils of life lie in finding purpose in having experienced them. By wondering why – and seeing challenges as opportunities for growth – I am confident that you, too, will find the motivation needed to persist in recovery.

CHAPTER 10

FALLING ON OUR BUMS

Question: *How does one go about writing a book on recovery when they feel as though they have fallen off their own pathway to it?*

Answer: *By accepting that falling on their bum is part of the process!*

When laying out the framework for this book, as is consistent with all my perfectionist doings, I organized all the chapters and titles in a cute little web, much like the ones we used to make in elementary school. Radiating outward from a central circle, inscribed with the title *From Emaciated to Emancipated,* were a variety of little spider arms, each filled with scribbled quotes and notes to help guide my writing. I devoted two hours every morning to tapping away on my keyboard, in addition to periodical afternoon blocks during which I could dive into some preliminary editing. I had a little Amazon Alexa device to keep me entertained and a lazy dog lying at my feet for comedic relief and companionship. All in all, I had great plans to pen a national bestselling recovery resource while simultaneously typing my way to personal health. However, what I neglected to prepare myself for were those dreaded disorder days, during which I had to forgo writing because it felt too hypocritical to guide others along a path off which I had fallen.

As it turns out, recovery is not about how well we dance around the cracks and crevices of our kooky or compulsive behaviors. It is about how we pick ourselves up when we trip over them. Thus, I want to reflect on my present struggles instead of hiding behind any wishful words of encouragement. I want to embrace the paralyzing anxiety that has kept me from pushing along on my self-imposed writing and recovery schedule. Yes, today I admit that I have fallen on my bum, but I do so in the hope that my hindrances may help us all move forward on this journey we call recovery.

The other day I had what I have come to refer to as a disorder day. A disorder day could be best summarized as that big, nasty step backwards that often follows those two teeny-tiny-yet-arduous steps forward. And disorder days happen. Accept them and remember that they do not negate our forward progress; instead, they allow us to find our footing so that we may continue in the right direction tomorrow.

"I feel like I am crossing a lake on thin ice during a blizzard," I said in response to my therapist's request to describe my *disorderly* recovery process. "I feel anxious all the time – as if I am listening to the ice crack below me with each step I take into the unknown. Despite my anxiety about the future, I have no choice but to move forward without knowing what's next because the blizzard surrounding me has distorted my vision. Not being able to see where I am heading, prepare for the next challenge or trust in the ground below me only adds to the unpleasantness of the present." I paused. I felt beaten down, yet not quite defeated. "But I am still walking!" I smiled. "Walking... and working hard to keep moving in a forward direction."

There are bound to be times when the ice cracks below us, and we have to backtrack a bit – but that should be perfectly acceptable in a society that prides itself on the "two steps forward, one step back" approach. There are also going to be times when we fall through the ice completely! However, every day that we shuffle our way across the slippery and uncertain surface of recovery, the more confident we become in our ability to navigate the terrain. We must also remind ourselves that we have the support of those who will pull us out of the frigid seas when we do fall through the ice – that is, if we allow them to.

We must have faith that the ice will continue to thicken as we trudge forward. As such, it is important to remain patient with the painfully slow pace of recovery (because moving too fast will likely cause us to fall flat on our faces), and we must be persistent in our continual forward progress (because sitting stagnant for too long at any one stage may well bestow us with a case of frostbite on our bums). Throughout it all, we must trust that the blizzard blinding our view of the opposing shoreline will let up because, in time, it will.

The other day, I tried to explain this same state of fragile existence to a caring coworker who's also an avid baseball fan. "Think of a strike zone," I told him. "On a 'normal' day, a 'normal' person has a pretty broad strike zone – that area over which a pitch can cross the plate and be considered hittable. When our strike zone is large, and life is going our way, we can handle a lot. We can be flexible when things don't go as planned and avoid having a panic attack if a pancake sneaks its way onto our breakfast plate."

He nodded. Whether it was because he understood my metaphor or he simply wanted to appease me for attempting, I am not sure. But regardless of whether others can relate to our state of recovery, it is essential that we accept the fact that things aren't particularly 'normal' for us right now. It is important that we don't get down on ourselves when our strike zone seems a little smaller than usual. It is important to accept that the person standing at the plate is not our coworker or therapist. It is you. It is I. It is we. And *we* need to accept ourselves, no matter what condition we are in.

I've been working hard to accept my stupidly small strike zone as of late – or, should I say, I've been working hard to accept myself, because the first step in recovery is self-acceptance. The strike zone will widen as we continue to work on our recovery; however, we must remember that recovery is work! So, for the time being, be gentle on yourself, and I will try to do the same. Accept yourself as you step up to the plate or onto the frozen lake that is recovery. Accept that the early stages of healing are not fun. Accept that your body is not going to feel good, that your head is going to hurt, and everything from your emotions to your excretory system is going to be erratic. Accept that you are not going to be exceedingly productive, playful or present for the time being – that is how it goes in eating disorder purgatory. However, always remember that, though it's impossible to skip over any of the many difficult stages of recovery, we do get to choose how long we stay in them! Be gentle on yourself but do continue to push yourself out of your comfort zone if you hope to make forward progress. Be content with who you are and where you are in this moment, but never be complacent in your journey forward.

So, with those two metaphors in mind, let's revisit this disorder day that I alluded to earlier in the chapter. I should have seen it coming after a surfing wipeout the week before had left my upper body immobilized by a strained chest muscle, but I didn't. I should have seen the red flags flying after skimping on, then altogether skipping lunch, but I didn't. Honestly, I should have known better than to go out surfing in the first place! My weight was still unhealthily low, and I was already on crutches thanks to an overuse injury in my Achilles tendon, a recurring issue caused by doing something that my body and psyche were not ready for: jogging!

So, there I was, forced to sit with my thoughts and struggles, literally and figuratively. It was frustrating. Over the course of the preceding weeks, my life had seemed to be getting more manageable. I was finally feeling like I was making progress. My clouded mind was starting to clear upon being fed – amazing how that works – and I was starting to reclaim my role as a functional human being. I didn't dread waking up every morning, nor did I have to rely on an Ativan prescription to get me through lunch every afternoon. My personality was beginning to resurface and, all in all, my metaphorical strike zone was widening. I was recovering!

But shit, if our paths aren't full of twists and turns! Thus, as is often the case, just as I felt like I was getting my head above water, a wave crashed over me and pushed me under again. I had metaphorically and literally wiped out!

To my credit, I made it through the first week of my injury in pretty good spirits. Little did I realize, however, that my damn deceitful disorder was subtlety working its way back to the surface. Slowly but surely, my anxiety was increasing, and the symptoms of malnourishment were beginning to show. I would stare blankly at my computer screen every time I tried to type, and I was having trouble focusing on conversations throughout the day. Even worse, my slightly dysfunctional digestive system had drifted into an all-too-familiar little ditty of diarrhea and constipation. (Sorry if this is too much information, but eating disorders are a bitch, and our bowels often take the brunt of it!) I could continue with a list of symptoms – some of which you'd know, while others are likely unique to my own obnoxious mind and body – but what it came down to was that Ed had snuck back into my life and grabbed hold of my soul.

Again, I don't know how I didn't see him coming. I don't know how I didn't realize that a stick of beef jerky didn't constitute a meal, or why I couldn't accept that my body burnt calories regardless of whether I went for a mid-afternoon surf or selected a more sedentary activity. I don't know why I couldn't comprehend that calories don't just magically appear in our systems, but that we have to consume them. I don't see how I didn't realize that walking with crutches exerted more energy than did a stroll without them... or that injuring myself (twice) was a blatant sign that I was not yet healthy enough to integrate exercise back into my life. For lack of better words, I don't know how I didn't see that I was fucking up. Actually, I do. I know exactly how I didn't see these things happening: I didn't see anything occurring around or within me because Ed had teamed up with my anxiety to build a barrier between the rational and reactive sides of my brain.

I recognize, though I can't quite fathom, that some of you reading this might never have experienced an anxiety attack of your own. Thus, to not to save all the insanity for myself, I thought I'd pause ever so briefly and attempt to put the emotions of one of my anxiety-ridden adventures into words for you. Keep in mind, however, that no word nor metaphor will ever adequately depict the nature of a true disorder day because the essence of anxiety lies in its inexplicability. Nevertheless, hold on tight because here we go!

The attack comes on quick, like a thunderstorm on a hot and humid July evening. An eerie stillness fills the air as I fall deep into a state of fearful introspection. There is no denying that the conditions are right for a thunderous eruption, and I am seized with uncertainty as to how I might best subdue the storm. Sometimes, I can hear the faint forewarning of an

encroaching attack far off in the distance, which gives me time to meditate,
paint or pray my anxiety away. Other times, it comes unannounced, like an
instantaneous flash of lightning or crack of thunder that sends my heart rate
soaring. Either scenario is paralyzing – and that paralysis is the difference
between anxiety and panic. Anxiety is the jaw-clenching tension that we
feel in anticipation of the storm. However, while anxiety is unpleasant and
can be extremely intense, it is at least addressable. Panic, on the other hand,
leaves us paralyzed in its wake.

There are several coping mechanisms that we might use to escape or
dissipate the storm – that is, if we are able to confront the source before
our anxiety turns to panic. For some, a few minutes of mindfulness or
meditation can quiet the thunder, while for others, it's calling a friend for
support that bows the rain. Unfortunately, there are bound to be times when
any attempt to alleviate our anxiety simply falls short and paves the way for
panic to slip in. In these instances, we are often left wet and worn down,
doing damage control while our most absurd thoughts and fears – as illogical
or insignificant as they may seem to an onlooker – become our reality and
pour down on us from every angle. We can't see. We can't hear. Everything
intensifies, and our senses are heightened beyond our ability to comprehend
what it is that we are truly feeling or experiencing. There appears to be no
way out because our perception of the real world is restricted to sporadic
flashes of lightning that light our way, as we scramble for shelter from the
storm while it wreaks havoc on us from above.

In the past, escape, for me, meant running. Quite literally, too,
because exercise had always provided the easiest "off switch" for
my anxiety. But I also ran metaphorically, because turning my back
on the disorder had always appeared a more attractive option than
facing it. Of course, there are all sorts of strategies out there to
help us respond to tense situations and intrusive thoughts in more
sedentary ways, but amid an anxiety attack, it is easy to resort to
old habits in an attempt to temporarily avoid or escape the situation
instead of facing it head on.

If there is a redeeming quality to these emotionally encapsulating
experiences, it would be that nothing of their level of intensity can
linger forever. Thank God! Eventually, we reach a point where the

emotional and/or physical exhaustion brought on by an attack becomes stronger than the attack itself. In that moment, the panicked storm that besieged us finally begins to fade, and in its place, a strangely unsettling stillness takes over. There's even a rainbow sometimes if we look hard enough! We are exhausted and drenched. We are broken and demoralized. But at least the storm is over – and for that we should be exceedingly grateful.

This storm metaphor might be good for depicting the devastation and dread that exists in our head; however, how about I leave you with a slightly simpler, somewhat silly metaphorical representation of the mayhem that is our anxious mind? After all, by this point in this book – or in your recovery – you are probably in need of a little lightheartedness to balance out the bad. That said, the best description for an anxiety attack that I have heard is that it's like a reverse orgasm: an all-encompassing experience that strips all the joy, love and euphoria from our existence, leaving us depleted, confused and utterly depressed. And, while we are at it, if an anxiety attack can be compared to a reverse orgasm, then think of panic as a chafing chastity belt!

I say all of this to emphasize that I am not recovered. I am in route, but there are plenty of anxiety-ridden days, during which the sound of my fingers tapping on my computer keys to write a book about recovery can make me feel like a hypocrite. Furthermore, I say all of this to remind you that my purpose for writing this book while still early in the recovery process is so that I may ride out the storm and share in the ecstasy of restoration with you. And sometimes, that simply means holding hands while we simultaneously seek shelter from the rain. I hope that my honesty empowers you to be open about your struggles too, because being vulnerable about our weaknesses in the present is what will allow us to reclaim our strength in the future. So, let us close out this chapter by acknowledging that opening our hearts to healing and our hands to holding might just be the key to turning a raindrop into a rainbow.

CHAPTER 11

ATTEMPTING TO BREAK OUR ENGAGEMENT WITH ED

It's often been said that when we stand with one foot in the past and one foot in the future, we piss on the present. Thus, although the years between my cycling sessions with Jack and meeting you in these pages were filled with many milestones and mishaps, let us avoid an unfortunate straddle by summarizing the remainder of the decade so that we can focus our attention on the present instead of peeing on it.

Jack had moved on to the great beyond, but his positive outlook on life remained very much alive in my soul and continued to push me to seek purpose beyond myself in the years that followed our fateful first ride. I was no longer able to compete at the professional level by this point, but my persistent love of endurance athletics prevailed and motivated me to launch a nonprofit program called Sweaty Sheep, which is still active today. It is a program that perpetuates Jack's playful spirit through our mission to utilize art and recreation as a way to mitigate the faith, social and economic barriers that divide our community. In other words, I dreamed up an organization aimed at bringing diverse people together through the power of play because maintaining a playful spirit has always been a foundational element of my recovery.

Upon graduating seminary in 2010, I was honored with the Presidential Homiletics Award ("homiletics" being nothing more than a fancy word for preaching), and quickly developed a passion for public speaking. As I started to publicly proclaim my somewhat untraditional view of religion, I came to find out that there were a lot of like-minded *unorthodox outsiders* in Louisville – and several of us united in the formation of our own un-church-y community. Unfortunately, my work in the nonprofit world was still not quite engulfing enough to distract me from my longstanding exercise addiction. Thus, it was during that time that I made a not-so-recovery-minded decision to accept a job as a personal trainer and endurance athletics coach at the local YMCA. This fitness-focused line of work would have been okay had my obsessive personality not pushed me to unhealthy levels, but we are who we are, and it didn't take long before I found myself secretly competing with my own clients and other gym-goers. Competition has often served as the crux of my compulsivity – be it restriction and/or over-exertion – and the comical part of this is that the people I am competing against often have no idea that they are in a competition! Ed's subconscious voice would push me to eat less than the dieters who'd come in at the start of the new year and run further than the marathoners who'd hit the treadmills during their lunch break. The problem was that those dieters would have a snack as soon as they left the gym, and those lunchtime runners would stop running after lunch. I, on the other hand, didn't know how to snack or stop.

It wasn't long after accepting that job that Ed also convinced me to dive back into the arena of endurance athletic competition, this time via the Ironman Triathlon (an absurdly unhealthy race comprised of a 2.4-mile swim, a 112-mile bike ride and a 26.2-mile run.) Unfortunately, my first few years of competition went pretty well – so well, in fact, that I launched my own coaching practice and picked up several sponsors to support my newest addiction. This is just another reason eating disorders are so damn difficult: because unlike other addictions, society likes to feed the egos of those who stop feeding themselves and encourage those who can't stop exercising to keep pushing onward.

"Man, you're lucky," friends would say when I shared about my struggles. "I wish I could be addicted to exercise or had the willpower to abstain from snacking! Do you have any diet tips for me?" Ugh. While our society scorns drug addicts and pushes abstinence on alcoholics, they praise our dependency to diet and exercise, and those words of encouragement only expand Ed's ego.

Of course, my past patterns proved consistent, and it didn't take long before my self-centered, endurance-athletic obsessions overshadowed the fulfillment I'd found in my church and nonprofit work. I hadn't fully forfeited my life to exercise – yet. Thus, over the course of those years, I managed to earn a second master's degree, launch a running program designed to help promote health in the city's homeless community and even attempt to dive back into the dating scene following a multi-year celibacy spree. Actually, the term "dive" may be a little bit too graceful a description of my disordered dating attempts during that time, so we should probably refer to them as "bellyflops" for the sake of accuracy. But that all changed when I met a cute brunette in the park one amazing autumn afternoon while I was out walking my dog.

"I see you out here pretty much every day," she said with a smile.

"Well, I own a condo on the corner," I responded, trying not to let my eyes give away my intrigue. "So, this is kind of my backyard."

"It's a pretty lonely backyard when your only companion is of the canine variety." A hint of sarcasm peppered her voice. "Just how many laps do you plan to take around the park with your four-legged friend before you ask me to join you?"

I melted. We've all been there. That moment when puppy love becomes larger than any of our disordered thoughts or daily agenda items. That moment when we forget about any addictions, anxieties or ailments and dream about our fairytale future instead. It is an awesome experience – and in contrast to my past engagements with the opposing gender, this one lasted more than a moment!

You may be wondering what made this relationship different than the disordered dating attempts of my past. Well, as it turned out, all those eating disorder issues that had interfered with my past relationships aided this one. Why? Because I had finally found myself a fellow *disorderee* to date.

It was match made in heaven! *Why hadn't I thought of this before?* I didn't have to worry about having to eat together because she also hated eating in public. I didn't have to deal with the anxiety of sitting still because we were both addicted to exercise. I didn't have to hide my compulsive behaviors because my equally kooky girlfriend had plenty of her own to match. It seemed I had finally found my soulmate! However, what I came to realize in the months that followed was that I was actually dating my disorder, not that cute brunette from the park. And, let me assure you, Ed is not someone that you want to get too intimate with.

Now, I've spoken to many addicts who met their soulmate in treatment and claim their overlapping recovery journeys helped them heal. These are successful couples whose bonds were built around a common addiction. So, what made our relationship different? Simple: ours was based on our common disorder, not on a shared effort to overcome it.

"What do you want to do today?" I asked one crisp fall morning in anticipation of a good hike or trip to the pumpkin patch. "I've got nothing on the schedule today other than you."

"Great! I'm up for anything!" Her energy and excitement flooded the phone. "I just finished a beautiful ten-mile trail run and I can be over in half an hour. I just have to shower."

"Oh, really?" My heart dropped. My day was just getting going after allowing myself a rare lazy morning. I had told myself the night before that I was taking a rest day, so I had awoken with no work or workouts on the agenda – that was, until my girlfriend told me about her morning jaunt. Now, all of a sudden, I was overcome by guilt and anxiety. *I can't see her,* I thought. *Not after she's been out running while I've been sitting around sipping coffee.* I panicked. "Actually, I just remembered that I have got some errands to run. How about we meet up at noon?"

"I thought you said that you had the whole day free?" The disappointment in her voice broke my heart. "But I guess noon will work."

I did not enjoy any of the 11 miles that I forced myself to run – notably further than her 10-mile trek – because I knew that, with each of them, I was living a lie. I couldn't soak in the colors of the changing leaves because my eyes were too busy scanning the park, making sure she wasn't around to see me "running errands." No,

I couldn't enjoy the day, nor the woman I wanted to share it with, because my exercise adultery had surfaced, and there was not enough space in my life for both my girlfriend and my disorder.

Over the course of the weeks to come, I began to pull away from a friend and partner whom I genuinely cared about, all because I felt the need to compete against her instead of cuddle with her. I became scared to touch her, talk to her or allow myself to love her. I was afraid to look into her eyes when we spoke because, within them, I saw my shadowy side – and I feared myself. We broke up several weeks later as a result of my pulling away; however, as I would come to find out, the emotional effects of my detachment, avoidance and lack of affirmation had already taken their toll...

"Hey, you!" I playfully answered the phone several years later. "I'm sure glad to see your name on my cell phone screen this morning." The two of us had recently reconnected, and we were working on rekindling our relationship.

"Um. This is *Gayle*, Ryan." Her mother's voice cracked on the other end of the line – and not because of bad cell service.

"Oh." I knew instantly that something was wrong, but I tried to be friendly. "What a pleasant surprise." It was a surprise alright, but any pleasantry was simply a superficial response to appease a possible future in-law.

"We found her in her apartment this morning." The voice on the other end transitioned from shaky to sobbing to silent.

Remember that age-old adage I'd mentioned earlier? That "trauma not transformed is transmitted"? Well, never have those words been truer than in that moment. More than five years have passed since I received that fateful phone call; however, I am still yet to open myself up to the idea of dating. Why? Because the truth is that I am still dating my disorder – and I am now all too aware of the danger of double-dipping.

It took some time and a good bit of therapy, but I was eventually able to accept the fact that I was not the cause of my former partner's suicide. That being said, it is undeniable that the emotional wounds that I unconsciously inflicted upon her by pulling away did not aid the situation.

So… am I destined to be single forever? I certainly hope not! However, before I can share my life and love with another person, I must first figure out how to take it back for myself. I must end one relationship before starting another – and the first person that I need to mend relations with upon doing so is myself. I hope that this story does not come across as demoralizing, but that it demonstrates the importance of loving oneself in route to loving another because we all deserve to experience love! We are each worthy of being loved, and we are all way too beautiful to give our attention to some deceitful, good-for-nothing disorder. So, the lesson here is this: Don't ever be afraid to open your heart up to another, but remember that, to do so, you must be willing to close it to the disorder first.

The Persian poet Rumi spoke often of love, and when making a metaphor for a successful relationship, he wrote about how "each column of a Cathedral must first stand strong on its own before ever supporting a structure beyond its being." Think about that one for a second. Are you far enough along in your recovery that you can stand tall on your own, or do you still rely on others (or some false fiancé named Ed) to hold you up? Do you seek to control what you eat, the numbers that show on your scale, your movement and/or your schedule in order to alleviate the anxieties of your day? Are you able to support and accept yourself for who you are, or is a relationship simply a means of seeking the acceptance that you lack? Upon answering these questions in the affirmative for myself, I returned to an anorexically fueled life of abstinence following that phone call – and, though I do yearn for companionship, I must first work on removing some of the false supports in which I've put my faith over the years. That way, I can practice standing straight and tall on my own.

CHAPTER 12

SHIFTING TO SANTA CRUZ

That's enough *rumi*nating on my past relationships, or ancient
Persian poets; however, I do promise to follow up with a sequel
to this story if/when I get my shit together enough to dive back
into dating. But at that point, I was once again single – and, upon
completing a second round of graduate school, retiring from the
Ironman circuit and experiencing a variety of good, bad and bizarre
times in Louisville, Kentucky, it was high time for a change of
scenery. Thus, I set sail for Santa Cruz, California – quite literally,
may I add, as I hoped to tap into my long-lost love for sailing as
a means of moving away from my addiction to swimming, biking
and running.

As much as I would love to claim that my westward migration
was fueled by intentions to further my recovery and pursue more
purposeful life goals, I haven't tiptoed around the truth thus far, and
I won't start now. So, let me be the first to admit that the real reasons
for my move were depression and exhaustion – or maybe exhaustion-
induced depression. Regardless of which of these unpleasant
emotions came first, my solution was the same. I was heading
for California – land of adventure, introspection and the prolific
professor Joseph Campbell, renowned for his timeless tagline, "Follow
your bliss." However, before packing up and heading west, I had a
few commitments to fulfill on the opposing coast, the first of which
involved my packing up and heading southeast.

I was at a pretty low point upon boarding a Florida-bound plane
one frigid February morning. I'd been asked to give the keynote

address at a conference on creative ministry, and although I felt very uncreative at that moment, I accepted the invitation in the hope that the salty sea breeze, along with a strong dose of St. Petersburg sunshine, would pull me out of my rut. Throughout the years, past to present, my routine-based lifestyle – a familiar characteristic of anorexia – has functioned as double-edged sword. While routine and structure are essential in easing my day-to-day anxieties, the depression that sneaks in when I feel trapped in a repetitious rut can be extremely debilitating. My inflexibility makes the more fulfilling experiences – such as travel or impromptu outings with friends – nearly impossible. At the same time, the fear of giving up my freedom keeps me ironically imprisoned in my own self-imposed compulsive tomb. These cycles are all the same. Repetition leads to restriction… restriction leads to depression… depression leads to overexertion… then, before I know it, I am, for lack of a better word, fucked. Thus, it was because of an all-too-familiar phase of feeling fucked that I anxiously boarded the airplane (after researching the all the supermarket and gym options available around my hotel in St. Pete, of course). I was a fraud, preparing to present on innovation under a false persona of creativity that I'd carefully crafted to cover up my rigid reality.

This feels like as good a time as any to dig a little deeper into the difference between ritual, routine and rut. If you've ever checked into residential care, you'll likely agree that most traditional treatment facilities revolve around routine. Each program that I have participated in has required my strict adherence to a set-in-stone daily schedule, a structure with which I quickly became comfortable – so comfortable, in fact, that I grew complacent. As a result, two problems repeatedly arise upon my leaving care. The first is that I struggle to function or feed myself when my day isn't laid out for me in tidy, time-sensitive, fashion – and I'll be damned if the real world doesn't like to shuffle our schedules! The second is that my fear of straying from these self-imposed routines leads me into a repetitious rut. I get anxious when my prescribed schedule gets stretched; however, I get depressed when my routine becomes monotonous. It's a "heads Ed wins; tails I lose" coin toss of mental health – and those are pretty unattractive odds.

This is where ritual comes in. By creating holistic rituals out of the otherwise repetitious elements of our day, we can add an element of mysticism to life's mundane moments. For example, I awake every morning at pretty much the same time to the same breakfast and same strong cup(s) of coffee. By pausing for a simple gratitude reflection before I grind my coffee beans, and by taking several mindful moments to truly taste each bite of my meal, I create an atmosphere in which appreciation reigns over anxiety and gratitude overshadows guilt. Try it, and you will find that appreciation tastes much better than anxiety first thing in the morning! Creating rituals out of routines is an easy first step in freeing yourself from the rut in which you're stuck. As you continue with your day, pause periodically to determine whether you are actively participating in a mindful ritual or following a mindless routine. If the latter is true, ask yourself how this activity serves you. If you still choose to follow through with it, do so only after taking the time to think about how you can be more present in it.

Now, back to the story. The vast majority of my first two days in Florida were spent walking (and sulking) endlessly along the clear blue water beaches of St. Pete. Unfortunately, I was unable to enjoy the sun and sand because I was too engulfed in self-judgment and obsessed with the calories I needed to burn before the buffet dinner opened – a dinner that I would wind up skipping because I felt too hopeless to mix and mingle with other ministers at the conference. So, instead of supper, I spent the evenings preceding my lecture hidden in a hot tub at the hotel, soaking in self-pity amidst an otherwise gorgeous sunset.

"Hey, mon! Whatcha doin' sittin' all lonesome-like while down here in paradise?" Never before has a happy Jamaican voice been as wounding as the one that met me, despite the playful innocence of his question. I looked up at this man's dreadlock-framed face, certain that misery was written on mine.

"I guess I just needed a little alone time," I said, hoping that he would take the hint and continue picking up the towels left around the pool by other patrons.

"That's no good, mon. You're a good-lookin' guy. Why do you sit all lonesome in this tub while cute bikinis are lining the bar?" His smile broadened. "Nope, no good at all."

"I guess I am just not in much of a mood to mingle," I mumbled. And my mood was darkening with every word we exchanged.

"Ya know what the problem is with you Americans?"

"What's that?" I cringed in preparation for a verse out of "Don't Worry, Be Happy," because we all know that there are no worse words to hear when dealing with anxiety or depression than "don't worry, be happy." However, what he said next would stick with me for years to come.

"You crazy Americans are so unhappy because you think and expect too much." He paused to allow the sincerity of his statement to shine through his smile. "Yep. You Americans expect way too much – but what'd it look like if, instead of expecting anything when you wake tomorrow morning, you simply *preferred* certain things to happen?" Without any further words of wisdom or even a salutation, he turned around and walked back into the sunset, leaving me mulling over his seemingly simple solution to life.

He was right. I have always expected a lot out of life. I wake up every morning – watch and calendar in sync – ready to engage in a preordained schedule that is overflowing with high expectations of how the day is supposed to unfold. I expect a certain breakfast at a certain time; a freshly ground cup of coffee that's pressed, not poured; ample time for a workout before work; and a brake-light-free commute. And anxiety engulfs me if any of these activities get interrupted. I expect my dog to behave a certain way, traffic to part as I drive through it, the supermarket to have each of my favorite foods, and all my meetings and agenda items to occur on time and without drama.

After hearing the Jamaican man's point of view, though, I made a conscious effort to release myself from expectations and to instead *prefer* certain things to happen when I awoke. I've come to accept that preferences are natural... we are, after all, human. Moreover, preferences aren't bad – they show passion. But freeing ourselves from expectation is essential if ever we hope to find peace and acceptance.

Eliminating expectations from my life has not been without flaw; however, by accepting that the world doesn't revolve around me (or my anorexic preferences), I've been able to make peace with some of life's unpredictable hiccups. So, the next time life throws you a curveball, how about taking a moment to breathe? A few short seconds to pause instead of panic? Then, once your heart rate returns to that of a functional human being, do your damnedest to smile as you mumble that Jamaican man's magical motto: "This is not what I preferred." Give it a try, if not for me, for that dreadlocked prophet of St. Petersburg!

I left Florida a little less depressed than when I had arrived. Now, it was time to leave Louisville. Packing up your entire life and moving across the country is not a simple task for anyone; however, it is exceedingly more difficult for someone struggling with obsessive compulsive tendencies and disordered eating. I knew that I had to get away from my community of type-A, endurance-athletic friends, and I hoped a physical move would make that escape a little easier. Unfortunately, without having made a conscious commitment to work on my disorder, the reality was that I was simply running from Ed once again… and, as luck would have it, Ed turned out to be quite the endurance athlete himself! Thus, for as invigorating as the change of scenery, schedule and social groups was, it didn't take long for me to adopt a coastal Californian version of the disorder I'd attempted to leave behind.

CHAPTER 13

CALIFORNIA DREAMIN'

In the early 1930s, New York native and existentialist philosopher Joseph Campbell took a sabbatical to the Golden State to study American society's shift westward. "I have come to believe that people are not looking for the meaning of life," he wrote upon his return, "in so much as they are looking for an experience of being alive."

Nearly a century later, I found myself following in Campbell's footsteps looking for just that: an experience of being alive. I yearned to experience life apart from the disorder that had distanced me from my friends, family and feelings of "aliveness" for 20-or-so years. I yearned to find inner peace and freedom. Simply put, I moved to California hoping to find hope. Well, I found it, but as those of you who read the introduction are aware that "hope is a dangerous thing. It can drive a person insane."

Why is hope so dangerous? Because it allows us to take a backseat in our recovery while dancing around our destinies – albeit with the most positive and hopeful of intentions.

Over the course of my decade spent in the Bluegrass State, I grew accustomed to being my own boss, setting my own schedule and enjoying the ease of mid-American life. Yes, outside of some self-imposed eating disorder difficulties, life in Louisville was pretty easy. The cost of living was cheap, the community was caring, and the external stresses of society seemed minimal in comparison to those in coastal California. What I found upon moving west was that life required a little more effort. It wasn't as though people were unfriendly; they simply seemed a little more serious than the laidback sun-and-surf bums that The Beach Boys sang about. The whole state seemed a little overly introspective – and the last thing an eating disordered mind needs is added introspection. It was as if everyone I met was on a search, as was I – a search for what it meant to be alive. However, all that introspection-seeking made the atmosphere a little intense, and I quickly became too serious in my search for an "experience of being alive" to actually *experience* life. I became too serious about life and not serious enough about the recovery process that would allow me to live it. Oscar Wilde offered up a little wisdom in this regard upon his declaration that "life is far too important to be taken seriously." However, what I have come to realize is that recovery is far too serious not to be.

Needless to say, I got the order mixed up somewhere westbound on Route 50 and pushed recovery aside in the hope that my eating issues would linger back in Louisville, so I could move forward with experiencing life in California. But damn, if that persistent, pain-in-the-ass friend of mine didn't hitchhike across the country in close pursuit. As a result, it didn't take long before I'd adopted or adapted Californian versions of past compulsive behaviors, and I failed in my quest to dim my eating disorder-derived depression with surfboards. In other words, I had built a foundation for my new life on the same shifting sands of my past.

Much like a sandcastle, my new Californian identity started out strong. I was able to find a sense of community in the surfing scene, a sense of purpose in a new job directing a gardening program for the homeless and enough excitement through the change of scenery to temporarily pull me out of my depressive cycle.

In retrospect, I am not sure how I didn't see the crash coming – literally! As irony would have it, it was another cycling wreck that sent me spiraling. I had been mountain biking at dusk and, idiotically, alone, when my front tire suddenly locked up on a log and heaved me over my handlebars. I cringed as I bounced across the trail's rocky surface and heard my collarbone and some of my ribs snap. I then proceeded to roll for a good distance before finally coming to a painful stop in a patch of sand, upon which I could assess my situation under a quickly setting sun. Luckily, I had just enough reception to call an ambulance, and just enough battery life left in my iPhone to utilize the flashlight feature to guide the search team my way. Unfortunately, I also had a good hour or so alone – save for the coyotes crying out all around me – to contemplate life and the struggles I knew awaited me upon my rescue.

In the months to follow, I put all my focus on my physical recovery instead of taking advantage of the downtime to work on my ED recovery. I could have worked with a counselor to address my anxieties; instead, I turned to chiropractors to realign my spine. Furthermore, as has been true in the past, I also resorted to restriction to compensate for my lack of mobility. So, while my malnourished bones slowly healed, my weight, mood and mental well-being took a plunge. It also became evident this time around that I was no longer in my 20s. I couldn't bounce back like before, and the physical abuse that I had inflicted on my body via a decade of restriction and over-exercising was beginning to show. Along with a few ribs and a collarbone, it seemed that my immune system had also broken. I could not stop getting sick. Little colds lingered for days... then weeks... then months. I constantly felt exhausted. My emotional and physical resilience were low, and that made otherwise insignificant stresses of life too much to handle. Little things, like a mid-day traffic jam or small shift in my morning schedule, would send me into an emotional upheaval. The worse I felt, the harder it was to eat – and the less I ate, the worse I felt. I eventually ended up being diagnosed with mononucleosis; however, at the time, I didn't know what was causing my strange symptoms.

In sum, I spent a solid two years feeling like donkey dung. I started having allergic reactions to things I'd never been allergic to (one of which, ironically enough, was cortisol); my excretory system became obnoxiously erratic (not that it was ever stellar); and I would regularly experience debilitating fatigue that made me fearful for the future. I had colonoscopies, endoscopies, ultrasounds and MRIs, but no one could figure out what was wrong. My heart rate was low, but not deadly, and I was diagnosed with gastroparesis (a common consequence of anorexia, characterized by slow digestion), but that did not explain my other ailments. In retrospect, my seemingly strange slew of symptoms could all be traced back to malnutrition, but, at the time, all I knew was that I was scared. Scared – and searching frantically for a magic pill that would fix me without my having to face reality and take responsibility for mending myself.

CHAPTER 14

THE DREADED DOCTOR'S APPOINTMENT

"How's your diet, Ryan?"

"My diet?" I parroted the question back while lying on the cheap paper covering the exam table during what was supposed to be a routine physical. My doctor was performing an EKG at the time, after my low heart rate had set off alarms on the computer that the nurse had used to take my vitals.

"Yes, Ryan. Your diet," she said while studying the squiggles on the EKG readout. "How much are you eating, and how much are you working out?"

"Um…" Reality hit me hard on that cold table, so I did what the disorder usually insisted I do. I started to lie. "Well, I eat three meals a day…" *minus the one or two I regularly skip.* "And I stay somewhat active…" *by working out five hours or so each day.* I wasn't trying to deceive her at the time, I just couldn't comprehend my own activity level or caloric intake. The only truth I could claim in that moment was fear – the fear of knowing that I was spiraling downward, coupled with the fearful reality that I could not slow the speed on my own.

"I'm scared," I blurted out after an uncomfortably long pause. It was the first time I had vocalized my fears.

She replied with words no patient wants to hear while lying on an exam table: "I'm scared, too." Then, she elaborated, "You've lost a bit of weight since our last visit… and you didn't have weight to lose! I need you to stop exercising for a while until we can get some pounds back on you."

The paralyzing effect that her comment had on me was all I needed to know that I was in trouble. *Stop exercising?* Despite how low my heart rate had been during the EKG, it suddenly spiked with her fateful command. *I don't know how to stop exercising.* I panicked. Suddenly, I felt alone. Alone and afraid. Alone, afraid and trapped. Trapped in my head. Trapped in my body. Trapped in the disease. I wanted to stop exercising. I wanted to lie on that exam table and never get up. It was safe. I knew that I could no longer live the way I had been, but I didn't know how *not* to. I simply knew that I was exhausted and scared – scared that, in a matter of minutes, I would have to walk out of the doors of that doctor's office and re-enter the real world alongside Ed.

"I think that I need help." My eyes welled up as those words as passed through my lips.

"There are a few online groups that may help you," she said with sincerity, but given the severity of my state of being, her suggestion seemed more like a mockery.

"No. I need real help." The floodgates opened and I began to weep. "I am scared. I'm scared of myself, and I need help."

"If you feel like you are going to hurt yourself, then you should go to the ER."

"I'm not suicidal!" I paused. I was not at a point where I wanted to take my own life – at least, not in the traditional sense. However, in reality, an eating disorder is nothing more than a slow and painful suicide. "I think I need to go into residential treatment." *Wait, what!? Did I really just say that?* I was shocked at the statement, despite having said it myself. This was supposed to be just another routine physical, but all of a sudden, I was sobbing and flailing for help.

"I think that residential care would be a good idea." My doctor looked up from her charts and into my tearful eyes. "Why don't we start looking at our options and check back in a few weeks" Then, with those words and a quick goodbye, she left the room.

"You are all good to go, Mr. Althaus," the nurse said as she removed the last of the EKG electrodes from my chest. "Just stop by the receptionist and schedule a follow-up visit on your way out," she added nonchalantly, as she rolled the machine out the door.

The truth was that I wasn't "all good." I was out of control. And I proceeded to prove that as I stepped out of that doctor's office with a prescription for rest and Reese's Peanut Butter Cups – and went directly to the gym instead, which was conveniently situated on the same street. It was lunchtime, and I was starving, scared and exhausted. So, I did what any logical human would do: I changed into my workout clothes. After all, if I was going to rest and eat, I had to burn off the excess calories I hadn't eaten at breakfast first.

CHAPTER 15

THE SELF-DESTRUCT BUTTON!

Congratulations, you have successfully made it through the slightly crazy, kind of kooky, cliff-noted summary of my past! Now, we can dive into the downfall that inspired me to start scribing this little book. We all have stories to share, and I hope that reading mine is helping you better understand your own. Furthermore, I hope that I did not bore, scare or scar you too badly thus far, because we are just now getting going with the good stuff!

> *"I'm scared."*
> *"I'm a little scared too,"* my doctor responded.

Do those words sound a little familiar? They should. You just read them in the last chapter. However, given they have been repeating in my mind for the past several months, I don't mind making you read them once more as well. This time around, though, I encourage you to do more than simply read them. Instead, I urge you to travel back to an instance in your personal life when you first came to terms with the reality that you needed help. What obstacles stood or stand in your way? What does "help" look like in your life? What small step can you take today that will guide you closer to receiving the help you need tomorrow? In other words, how can you help yourself get help?

> *"... I need help."*
> *"There are a few groups around town that may help you."*
> *"No. I need real help. I am scared of myself, and I need help..."*

As it turns out, there are immense differences between knowing you need help, asking for help, getting help and helping yourself. Sadly, far too many of us get lost in the gaps in between these actions, and, as such, we often fail to act. I needed help, and I needed it right then! At the time of that visit, I was 36 years old, stood at 6 feet tall, weighed in at 138 pounds, and had a resting heart rate of 40 beats per minute. To the oblivious onlooker, I was skinny, but not horribly unhealthy. My heart rate was slow, but not deadly. And, while I was indeed a little kooky, I hadn't quite gone batshit crazy... yet. This is because the eye of the oblivious onlooker couldn't see the disease eating away at my soul, psyche and body from within.

Well, the month to follow that not-so-routine physical turned out to be the most difficult month of my life. And when I finally landed in an ICU bed some four weeks later, I weighed 121 pounds, and my broken heart beat a mere 24 times per minute.

Question: What the hell had happened?

Answer: It was a common disordered phenomenon known as self-destruction.

I knew upon leaving that doctor's office that I needed to enter residential treatment; however, for me to do so, Ed had me convinced that I first needed to be the sickest I could possibly be. This is an all-too-common, and idiotically ironic, reality. We address our fear of surrendering control to a team of well-trained doctors, focused on restoring us to health, by first fully surrendering control to a disorder that is hell-bent on killing us. And damn, if that disorder won't try!

Any number of obstacles can inhibit us from seeking and/or receiving help. For example, as a guy with an eating disorder, I found that my residential options were halved from the get-go, based solely on my sex. Add to that the insurance hurdles, the process of receiving medical clearance (you have to be the perfect amount of ill – not too sick, but just sick enough), and finding the time needed to take a month or more off of life, and we are left with a seemingly insurmountable wall to scale in route to treatment – a wall which must be faced while already in a state of physical, emotional and mental depletion!

As much as I would prefer to sweep my memories of those weeks into the distant recesses of my mind, selective amnesia wouldn't be of much help to any of us. So, with that in mind, I invite you along for a field trip into my manic mind as I recount one of my more average, anxiety-ridden, self-destructive days that followed my fateful visit to the physician – in anticipation of my eventual, inevitable return to residential treatment.

***

The day would start with the buzz of my alarm – well before sunrise – at 5:50am. Actually, my day usually started much earlier than that, as I would lay wide awake in the middle of the night, fearing another day. Nevertheless, at 5:50, I'd drag myself out of bed and stumble outside for a few sun salutations. My body constantly ached from overuse and self-abuse, so it seemed only logical to start the day by stretching my starved and strained muscles. After a little yoga, I'd head back in for breakfast, which I'd eat in the dark, shriveled up in an anxious ball next to my space heater. It was June at the time, but I was always cold, and the comfort that my heater provided was one of the preciously few calming aspects of my life to which I could cling. As for my morning meal? I would generously call what I consumed "breakfast" because the food that I prepared constituted a meal. However, as it turns out, there is a difference between preparing food and eating it. Thus, in that regard, it's more accurate to say that I would sit and look at breakfast for a while before continuing my morning. I was starving, but too exhausted to trust that I would have the energy to exercise off any calories I consumed – so, just to be safe, I'd simply not eat. Unfortunately, the panic signals that my body was sending in response to being starved were about as energizing as a gallon of Red Bull; thus, my absurd anxiety, coupled with a good dose of caffeine, would fuel the day's workout despite my empty tank. True, I may have skimped or skipped breakfast, but I would never dare do the same with my morning coffee! So, before biking to the harbor for a three-hour paddle, I would infuse (or abuse) my body with several strong cups of caffeinated mud – a beautifully acidic addition to an anxious and empty stomach.

Now, for most, a morning kayaking adventure lit by a slowly rising sun – a peaceful Pacific paddle through the Northern Californian fog, alongside barking seals and an occasional humpback whale – would sound pretty incredible. And, indeed, it would have been incredible – had I been present enough to see through the fog of my eternal panic attack, that is! Upon pulling my kayak out of the water a few hours later, I would bike back to my computer to try and get some work done. Well, that was after taking an hour-long detour to pedal off any excess calories that still might be lingering from the breakfast that I didn't actually eat. In other words, I had to make room for the imaginary lunch I'd splurge on by exercising off the breakfast that I had merely *thought* about eating.

Any attempt to work at this point was a waste of time because my exhausted eyes could not focus on a computer screen long enough to make it through an email. I was tired – so tired, in fact, that I would venture back to the water for a plunge into the icy Pacific in the hope that the cold water would shock me into a state of alertness. Unfortunately, *alert* also meant *anxious* — and since I was already in the water, Ed's voice would whisper, "Why not aqua jog your mid-afternoon anxiety away, Ryan?" I couldn't actually jog by this point because my quadriceps had atrophied to the point that they could no longer support my body if I ran on solid ground, so running in the ocean provided a convenient alternative. By the time I finally got back to my computer, the workday was over (as if it had ever started), so I would scroll through a list of friends on my phone to see if I could find a walking partner. I would assure myself, *Walking isn't actually exercise; I am simply being social. Just a healthy stroll with a friend, right?* Well, by the time we ended that "healthy stroll," all the not-so-healthy, calorie-consuming activities of my day were all but forgotten. Still, my compulsory, competitive spirit would make one more appearance and insist that I had to out-move and under-eat all my friends, neighbors and coworkers – even my dog. Fortunately, the spin bike that I kept in the garage provided an easy way to do so! But like the walk, it wasn't exercise in my mind – just a quick spin, followed by a little more yoga, to loosen up my aching body before dinner.

By the time I had spun, stretched, showered and fixed dinner, it would be nearing midnight, and I'd be starving. I knew from experience that I couldn't control my eating once I started when I was this hungry, so, just to be safe, I would fill my plate with absurd amounts of fruits, veggies and air-popped popcorn to try and be gluttonous without too much guilt. I have always felt guilty for eating. Maybe that is why I've always loved the sensation of starvation so much: It is one of the few feelings that I can count on – and induce myself – to free me from my self-disgust.

I would finally collapse on my bed around 1am – and good God, was I exhausted! Unfortunately, despite not having the energy to lift my head off the pillow, I couldn't sleep because of malnourishment, my late-night binge and the anxiety of knowing I'd have to start the same suicidal sequence in less than six hours. I am not sure what was worse, really: indigestion or the anxious anticipation of my obnoxious alarm clock, which would ring just before dawn so that I could repeat my ridiculous routine again the following morning.

***

Did I mention that this was a *normal* day in the life of my self-destructive disorder? The truly scary thing was that, in my mind, it made perfect sense, and the anxiety I felt throughout that month provided more energy than any amount of food ever could. Furthermore, if my activity level wasn't absurd enough, my reasoning sure was. I would push myself to keep moving all day because I felt guilty sitting still, but then I would lie about my exercise habits because I was too embarrassed by my addiction to let others in on it. In other words, I felt guilty when I wasn't doing what I felt guilty for doing (exercising), all the while feeling guilty for consuming food that I was not consuming. True, the whole thing seems pretty damn illogical when put to print; however, illness as a prefix easily negates logic – it's ill-logic-al. Thus, knowing that I was heading for another round of residential treatment, I would let Ed make my decisions for me until my body gave out on me. And it did.

CHAPTER 16
ICU ADVENTURES

"Wow!" The triage nurse double-checked the wiring on the heart rate monitor. "I need a gurney!" she shouted. "And ASAP – he's showing a heart rate of 24 with a blood sugar reading of 28." Then, as if I hadn't heard her frantic yells, she turned back toward me with the sincerest smile she could muster and soothingly said, "I want you to sit nice and still, dear. Are you dizzy?"

"No." I wasn't dizzy – not in that moment, at least, though that's most likely because I had gotten used the feeling. I studied the look of concern in my nurse's eyes before eventually admitting that I had passed out in the shower the night before. I was only out for a few seconds, but the experience proved scarier than my fear of being strapped to a stretcher, so I'd arranged for a ride to the hospital the following day. At the time of this ER exchange, it had been a little over a month since that fateful visit to my doctor during which I first admitted that I needed residential treatment. After that, I had lost more than 15 pounds, along with any semblance of sanity, somewhere amidst the pain-in-the-ass process of getting help.

"Here we go!" An aide rolled in a stretcher a few seconds later. I couldn't help but appreciate the irony in their urgency. For more than a month, I had been begging for a referral into an inpatient treatment center, but I was brushed aside and given links to online support groups instead, effectively silencing my pleas. Now, after about 100-or-so dead-end phone calls, four weeks of fearful nights alone and a friend dropping me off at the ER in a last-ditch attempt to get help from a health industry that likes to ignore mental illness until it becomes deadly, I wasn't even allowed to climb onto the gurney by myself for fear that my heart might stop beating.

"Are you able to stand up long enough that we can get you on the stretcher?"

"Sure," I snickered under my breath. I had power-hiked ten miles along the cliffs of Santa Cruz before going for a quick swim just a few hours earlier, trying to override the anxiety of this ER visit. Thus, standing up for a few seconds didn't seem like too horribly hard a task.

I hadn't so much as gotten my butt off the chair before three pairs of hands grabbed ahold of me and placed me – a little less than gently – on a shiny silver stretcher. Within seconds, I was rolling through the hospital's halls with a heated blanket draped over me and an array of wires streaming from my bare chest. I had surrendered, and for that reason, I had a chance at survival.

Surrender is a strange and scary term in our slightly crazy, control-seeking, compulsive eating disorder vocabulary. In fact, I recently bought a book entitled *Trust, Surrender, Receive*, and those three words have been swirling around in my mind ever since. Trust is a high first hurdle, and as I grow increasingly aware of the deceptiveness of my disorder, I have realized that I have never been able to trust myself to make healthy decisions. I've had to admit that I am unable to trust my body and the feelings of hunger or fullness that tell me when to eat, what to eat and when to stop. I cannot trust that my body knows itself better than my mind thinks it does, and that this same body will figure out its own optimal weight when fed correctly. I cannot trust that a period of weight restoration will not spiral out of control and leave me in a 300-pound pickle. Finally, I have never trusted that I could be a happy and healthy human being at any weight (300lbs included), which is sad because, as it turns out, weight and happiness are *not* dependent on one another. All said and done, I have never trusted myself; thus, I have never been able to surrender to recovery or receive the help that might guide me to it.

The intensive care unit (ICU) was different, though. I didn't have to trust myself in order to surrender. This was essential because, at that point, the only way that I knew how to surrender was to give complete control over to another. I couldn't surrender for a meal, knowing I would have to dive back into a normal day thereafter. I couldn't surrender to a day of outpatient treatment, knowing that I would be alone with myself that night. I either had to surrender my entire existence or nothing at all – and after a few weeks of asking for support had exhausted my inhibitions, I finally surrendered in the hope of receiving help.

Will I ever be able to trust myself? Will I ever feel worthy of receiving help, love or food? Will I ever figure out what surrender means outside of my addiction-oriented, all-or-nothing approach to life? Will I have to spend the rest of my life bouncing between residential treatment centers, or will I finally figure out how to healthfully reside with myself? Those are all big, anxiety-inducing questions – and the only thing I have ascertained on my journey thus far is that we don't need to answer them all to start on the path of recovery.

> *Be empty of worrying*
> *Think of who created thought!*
> *Why do you stay in tomb when the door's so wide open?*
> *– Rumi*

Surrendering sucks, but it is a whole hell of a lot more freeing than the alternative. So, for as physically and emotionally empty as I felt upon entering the ICU, doing so allowed me to empty myself of worry for the first time in a long time. I felt a strange sense of peace and freedom amidst the beeps, blinking lights and locked doors of the unit. Was it pleasant? Hell no! I was alone and depressed in an ICU bed with my disordered thoughts! However, despite any of the obvious unpleasantries, I didn't have to worry. I just had to *be*. I didn't have to think. I just had to surrender to what Rumi deemed "that which created thought." As a result, I was able to use that time to look inward at my fearful soul through the entryway of my self-imposed ED tomb. And all I had to do was figure out how to step through that "open door," instead of rolling boulders in front it.

I wish I could claim that the worry-free feeling I experienced in the ICU remained when I resumed my life outside the hospital several weeks later, but, well… let's just say that fear has a way of fucking with our freedom. Take that as a foreshadowing, if you will, and flash-forward with me for a moment as I make a metaphor out of one of the more interesting exchanges that occurred in my early days of freedom. Worry not, we will pick back up where we left off with my ICU adventures shortly, but for now, kick back and enjoy a little time-traveling…

***

"I need this boat," declared a young man from the deck of a 35-foot schooner that I was selling. I had returned to Santa Cruz only a few weeks earlier, following 16 days of intensive inpatient treatment, and I was quite grateful to be slicing through the waves of Monterey Bay on my sailboat once again. "I want to buy it."

"That's good, because it is for sale." I smiled. It was an obvious response given that we were out for a sea trial at the time; however, the strain in his eyes told me that the conversation we were about to have would be about something other than the boat.

"Can I tell you a story?"

"Um. Sure…" I hesitated a little. Admittedly, I wasn't in the mood for stories at the time. It'd only been a week or so since I'd stepped back into the real world, and the stresses of catching up on life, coupled with the incessant internal eating disorder dialogue in my head, had left me feeling understandably antisocial.

"You're a minister, right?"

"Yes…" I paused. That question always makes me nervous when it precedes a conversation because there is no way to censor the confessions that often follow it.

"Listen. Ten years ago, I made a bad decision – a choice that put me behind bars for the last decade of my life." He pulled up his left pant leg to reveal an ankle monitor that kept him captive amidst an otherwise open ocean. "I made a bad decision, and because of it, I am never going to be free."

"We all make bad decisions," I said, trying to comfort him and encourage him to continue with his story.

"The only way that I will ever be free is to relinquish my US residency and sail to another country." He paused. "I want to sail to Fiji."

"Oh." I tried to stay open-minded, but given that this kid had started our sail by stating that it was only his second time on a sailboat, open-mindedness was a little bit difficult. "You want to single-handedly sail a 35-foot boat across the Pacific Ocean?" A subtle smile snuck across my face. "Without knowing how to sail?"

"Well, yes." The sternness of his stare told me that he was beyond serious. "I could set off next week if you sell me this boat and teach me the basics."

I was speechless. His openness to adventure, though slightly suicidal, made me jealous. There I was, free to set sail whenever, and to wherever, my heart desired. Free to wander the world without having to share my whereabouts with a parole officer, parent or partner. But while my ankles remained free from of any monitors, I remained locked inside a self-imposed prison. Physically, I was free to drop everything and set off for adventure at a moment's notice; however, I was entombed by an eating disorder of which I was beginning to grow damn tired. It was, from this state of emotional imprisonment, that I peered into the adventurous eyes of a young man whose soul was free to escape and explore the world, but whose body was held captive by society. In the words of eating disorder recovery advocate Alanis Morissette, "Isn't it ironic, don't you think?"

***

That story remains heavy on my heart for two reasons. First, as much as I'd love to say that the young man bought my boat and sailed his way to Fijian freedom, it turned out that his parole officer caught wind of his plans (that pun was intended), and he quickly ended up behind bars again. Second, the experience made me realize the parallels between Rumi's description of freedom and my own life. "Why do [we] stay hidden away in [our] tomb when the door is so wide open?" It had been a hypothetical question upon my first read, but one that lingers in my soul because of the reality of it. It is also a message that is reiterated in the band Mumford and Sons' 2009 hit, "Roll Away Your Stone." Unfortunately, copyright laws keep me from sharing the lyrics with you in print; however, ask your nearest smart speaker to play the tune so that you might reflect on how the words apply to your own recovery journey.

In my case, that song became my theme throughout those weeks spent in residential care, and it remains my go-to tune for impromptu self-empowerment dance parties with my dog. FYI, I have discovered that the best means of freeing oneself from the depressive thoughts that come with those aforementioned disorder days is to dance and sing our way back to sanity. As such, I highly recommend creating a recovery playlist of your own – and always keeping it within earshot! That way, when the worries of the world get you down, you can find assurance in the mere fact that a song such as "Roll Away Your Stone" exists because it means that you are not alone in feeling the feelings it expresses.

With one or two of those recovery tunes setting the tempo, take a moment to list out all the things that keep you imprisoned in your tomb. Is it an eating and/or workout regimen? Is it a fear of gaining weight? Is it a fear of or addiction to a scale or mirror? Maybe worries over the caloric differences between white and wheat bread make you wince… or perhaps deciding which condiment you're "allowed" to smear on that slice makes you shiver? Whatever it is, I have found that acknowledging my many "ankle monitors" makes confronting them a little less intense.

Okay, now that you have a few your own stones fresh in your mind, pause to ponder which of these worries you might roll away today – like, right now. My therapist refers to this as "picking the low-lying fruit." Which of your behaviors is most within reach at this moment? This is a fantastic way to start each morning. Try it tomorrow! Instead of waking up and diving into the depths of your disorder, what if you faced off with one of the more feasible fears? What if you approached tomorrow with a plan of attack so that Ed couldn't ambush you as you bit into your bagel… or so that you would have the confidence to bless yourself with something so joyous as a bagel?!

CHAPTER 17

AN IMPATIENT INPATIENT

I had a lot of time to think through my list of high- and low-hanging fruits during the 36 hours I spent lying in an ICU bed; unfortunately, nothing good comes from idle thought. I tried to distract myself with movies, but I couldn't concentrate on them. I dove into a novel, but after rereading the same first page about 50 times, I ended up throwing it across the room in a fit of foggy-headed frustration. I even played Picasso and painted a pathetic picture of the sailboat that I mentioned in the preceding chapter. Sadly, though, each stroke of my brush only pushed me deeper into depression.

How did I allow this to happen? How am I going to get my life back? The thoughts continued to spiral in a downward direction as I assessed my situation. *What is it that I am even living for?*

"It's dinner time, Mr. Althaus." The nurse snapped me out of my depressed daze. "We have meatloaf with mashed potatoes or pasta. Are you hungry?"

I let loose a laugh. Talk about adding insult to injury! There I was, lying in an ICU bed because I'd about starved myself to death, and I was now being teased with mashed potatoes?

"How about some of that infamous hospital Jell-O?" I responded, sounding slightly sarcastic, but secretly craving the jiggly dessert.

"We can do that." She smiled. "Regular or sugar-free?"

It was a milestone moment. I had a choice to make. That nurse had unknowingly dangled some low-lying fruit in front of me – quite literally, as the Jell-O had pineapple pieces in it! Now I had to decide if I was going to grab it. *What should I do? Regular Jell-O – full of fructose and refined sugars – or sugar-free and safe?* It was a monumental moment, in terms of motivation. Was I ready to do the work to get well, or had I succumbed to treatment in the hope that someone else might fix me? I knew that, starting the next morning, I'd be force-fed six meals a day, but I also knew that recovery couldn't start with forced feeding tomorrow... it needed to start with my choice to get well right then. It needed to start in that moment. It needed to start in that ICU bed with a sugar-sweetened snack.

"I'll take one of each," I blurted out, after an eternity of indecisiveness. I'd done it! I made a choice! And that decision was quite revolutionary because it proved to me that recovery did not have to be an either/or topic. We have options – and with options come the power to choose. And finally, I had chosen recovery.

"Great! Let me fetch those for you." The nurse let loose a little giggle as she glided out of the room, completely oblivious to the major U-turn she had just inspired.

Despite the unpleasantries of the ICU and my artificially sweetened supper selection that evening, I remain quite grateful for my stay there. For one thing, being forced to stay off my feet for a day or so allowed me a chance to get my footing back after what could best be defined as a month-long panic attack... and, good God, did I ever need the rest! By the time I made it to the ER, I had lost all ability to think clearly or speak sanely, and I couldn't be trusted to be alone. I had been a moderately professional and seemingly put-together human being a few months before, but I had suffered a complete mental and emotional breakdown. I had officially relapsed – and that short ICU detour gave me the chance to come to terms with my state of being before diving into inpatient ED treatment. In less eloquent words, I'd fallen off my flipping rocker and needed to sit in timeout with myself for 36 hours to reassess my life and my actions.

It was during that intensely introspective time in the ICU that I was finally able to come to terms with the severity of my situation. Whereas body dysmorphia had allowed me to pass by mirrors and pretend I was healthy in the outside world, I couldn't mute the alarms triggered by my low pulse rate on the hospital's heart monitors. Oh, and don't think I didn't try! I nearly broke a $10,000 machine around 2am one night when I started pulling plugs and pushing buttons in a feeble attempt to silence its incessant beeping!

No, I couldn't pretend that everything was peachy while a team of a nurses kept checking in on me to make sure my low blood sugar hadn't sent me into a coma. I couldn't ignore much of anything in the ICU. I couldn't deny the fact that I would likely die if I didn't decide to get better. As such, it was while lying there in ICU isolation that I came to an incredibly empowering conclusion: Despite the pain of living as of late, I did not actually want to die. Somewhere, deep inside, I had hope that I could recover – and this is an essential realization in recovery.

For so grateful as I was for that ICU detour, I was even more grateful that it only lasted 36 hours! The only problem was figuring out where to go from there. My insurance company was not affiliated with any inpatient eating disorder programs in the area, and ICU beds were not only expensive, but in exceedingly high demand, given that this happened at the height of the COVID-19 crisis. However, just as I was about to lose hope, one of the case managers told me about a newly opened psychiatric center that had just begun to accept severely anorexic patients.

So, that was it: I was officially admitted to a psych hospital and, therefore, I was rolled out of the ICU and down the hallway wearing nothing but a not-so-flattering paper gown... but, hey, at least it wasn't a straitjacket!

CHAPTER 18
SANITY? WHAT'S THAT?

"Welcome to Fremont, Mr. Althaus." The intake nurse seemed sincere enough in his salutation to elicit my trust. "You're one of our center's first eating disorder patients, and, given how excited the team is to learn from you, I have no doubt that you will get plenty of attention!"

"Oh, um, great… I think." Before I could decide whether my anorexic uniqueness was a good or bad thing, one of my soon-to-be-neighbors came flying through the doorway wearing only a sliver of his hospital gown.

"Hare Krishna!"

"Blessings indeed, *Evan*." The intake nurse shot a smile in my direction before turning his gaze back to my new friend. (Oh, and let me not fail to mention that the sliver of gown that Evan wore was covering his head, not blocking our view of his bum!)

"What do you say you go back to your room and wait for Krishna to come while I finish checking in our new resident?"

"Hare Krishna!" he continued to shout, as he skipped down the hallway and back into his doorless dormitory room.

"We have a *diverse* group here," the nurse continued, as if nothing out of the ordinary had just occurred.

In the days to follow, I found the diversity of the unit to be a welcome blessing. From dementia to schizophrenia to PTSD to Tourette's, the unit proved to be a healing hodgepodge of mental illnesses, where my eating afflictions were just another entry on a long list of disorders. Furthermore, in contrast to the seriousness of the ICU, my comrades in the psych unit proved to provide pleasantly comical company, and I began to find comfort in our community. True, the clan (myself included) could be kind of kooky on occasion, but none of that mattered because everyone was authentic and accepting. The liveliness and lightheartedness provided a much-needed reprieve and stood in stark contrast to the intensity and isolation of the past month. All in all, the psych hospital provided a beautiful transition between the ICU and residential care. Was it pleasant? Hell no! I was in an insane asylum! However, I was safe, I was out of the ICU, and, for the moment, I was entertained.

"You must be Ryan." A soft voice pulled my attention away from my scribbles.

"I am," I replied, as I peered up at the tall figure that stood before me.

"I'm Jeff." The stranger took a seat beside me. "I was told you wanted to meet with me. I am the chaplain here."

"Oh! Great! Thanks for coming." I set down my crayon and, with a slightly sarcastic smirk, said to the clergyman, "I must admit, I like your seat better."

"Oh, um…" The initial confidence of his voice softened with uncertainty. "Well, we could switch if your seat is uncomfortable."

"Ha! No need — our chairs are both the same." All the furniture in the unit was sterilized, standardized and heavily weighted to prevent it being thrown across the room. "My discomfort doesn't come from the literal seats we are sitting on." I adjusted myself on the chair to emphasize my point. "It's actually the role of patient that I'm uncomfortable with." I paused again, but this time to adjust my outlook on the situation, not my position. "A couple of weeks ago, I was actually a moderately sane Presbyterian minister who, ironically enough, had served as a psych chaplain during graduate school!"

"Really?" His politeness curbed his curiosity enough to keep him from asking the question that we both knew was on the tip of his tongue: *What the hell happened!?*

It was a question I'd been asking myself for days by that point, but then, the nametag on this man's neatly pressed shirt triggered a flashback to the conversation that I had shared with a different chaplain some 20 years before. The answer hit me: "The purpose of life," she had said, "is to find purpose in living."

So, what the hell happened?

Easy. I had lost my why. I'd lost my sense of self and purpose. I'd lost myself, and upon realizing it, I began to weep. Now, crying was nothing too out of the ordinary by this point – in all honesty, most of my days in the psych hospital were interspersed with a midday sobbing session or two; however, it was during this particular episode that I first started to see my tears as a source of empowerment, rather than a sign of self-pity. I began to see my teardrops as prisms that could color the life waiting for me outside those concrete walls, rather than as consequences of my imprisonment within them. I held fast to the spirit of this revelation throughout the remainder of the morning, then, following lunch, I commandeered my trusty carton of Crayola crayons and drew a picture of a teardrop-shaped rainbow to serve as the fitting backdrop for a poem about the transformation of my tears into rainbows. And, though I am admittedly not a poet, I would love to share it with you:

> *Cherish thee, oh blessed tear,*
> *Though seen by most through a lens of fear;*
> *Instead, a prism allowing the heart to clear,*
> *And a sign a rainbow is drawing near.*
>
> *Yes, blessed we are by these salty droplets,*
> *Spices of life singing soulful sonnets.*
> *Filled with spirit and poetic flow;*
> *Joy or pain – in every tear, an opportunity to grow.*
>
> *So, cherish indeed these signs of struggle;*
> *Of brokenness, of pain and trouble –*
> *Because by escaping eyes once shattered to rubble,*
> *The gifts they promise are more than double.*

One other pouting session also stands out as both pitiful and empowering from my time in the unit, so, despite its slightly embarrassing context, allow me to relive the story.

Breakfast had been a challenge that day. I'd been served a syrup-smothered stack of pancakes, a side of sausage and a bowl of sherbet. Yes, you read that right: SHERBET! For breakfast! Ice cold, sugary, sherbet – just sitting there, mocking me alongside a heaping hunk of fried pig! Needless to say, the meal was far from pleasant, but I managed to power my way through it after my nutritionist promised I could have a fresh fruit cup for my snack. However, much to my chagrin, that nutritionist snuck off before snack time! So, when an unsuspecting nurse set an Otis Spunkmeyer muffin in front of me, I erupted.

"The nutritionist promised me fresh fruit!" I yelled at the nurse. "This is *so* not fruit! And it is very, very far from fresh!"

"It is a blueberry muffin," the nurse said with a hint of sarcasm. The staff had grown accustomed to my mealtime meltdowns by this point and seemed to enjoy teasing me. "Oh, and your nutritionist also added strawberry jelly and butter." She smiled as she slid two small plastic containers my way. "That makes for two fruits: strawberries and blueberries."

"Neither of those count as berries! And who the hell puts butter and jam on a greasy, sugary muffin!?" I continued to complain, despite knowing damn well it wouldn't get me anything but a supplement. Oh, and supplements, for those of you blessed not to know, are pretty much those meal-replacing mock milkshakes given to old folks in nursing homes. And, although my grandma had always enjoyed the chalky chocolate ones, I'd personally rather throw the stupid Otis Spunkmeyer muffin into a blender, along with its side of butter and jam, and drink that instead.

"Does that mean that we will not be eating snack today?"

I couldn't speak. I was furious – so, in lieu of a response, I simply stared at the plate while tears formed in my eyes. It'd been two days since I had missed a meal, but that menacing little muffin was messing with me.

"You only have four minutes left before I have to serve you a supplement." The nurse glanced casually at her phone before diverting her attention back toward the movie that was playing to entertain the residents. It was one of my old-time favorites,

Mrs. Doubtfire. However, as much as I love Robin Williams, I had yet to reclaim my laughter, so I had chosen to spend my morning putting together a puzzle in isolation instead.

But then, with a mere three minutes left, I was stricken with a humbling realization: No one cared! I was throwing a passive-aggressive fit as an F-U to nurses who were simply counting down the minutes until they could clock out, go home and – quite likely – *enjoy* a muffin or two of their own. All the stress that I had placed on my little muffin meltdown was simply the result of my ego's insistence that the world actually cared if I ate snack. I glanced up at the clock on the wall. Two minutes now. I had two minutes left to answer an incredibly important question: Did I want to get well for me, or was I doing this for someone else? If the latter was true, I knew that I was in trouble because none of the nurses, doctors or staff really cared about my muffin conundrum. Now, that is not to say they didn't want to see me get better, but rather that the only one that was truly impacted by the decision to eat the muffin was me.

"Hey!" the Hare Krishna kid broke my pathetic, pastry-induced silence. "Can I have that muffin if he isn't going to eat it?"

"No!" I yelled as I smeared butter and jam across the glistening surface of the muffin. My abrupt response had startled the nurse and the Krishna kid – though they each began to cheer me on as I bit into my blueberry nemesis. I looked around the room as I chewed, and it was then that my situation truly began to fall into perspective. There I was, a privileged American anorexic guy, pouting over a muffin that millions of starving people all over the world would pay a day's salary to savor. Yep, I was an emaciated orthorexic – ignorant to true hunger – whining because he was forced to eat refined sugar instead of fresh fructose for snack.

"Good job," the nurse said nonchalantly as she cleared the empty plate and strolled back to her station.

"Yeah! Good job," added the Krishna kid as he followed in her footsteps with high hopes of procuring a muffin of his own.

I was emotionally exhausted. The intensity of the muffin encounter had depleted me. But something important had happened during my breakdown: I realized that the world didn't care what

I ate, what I weighed or what crazy compulsive or restrictive thoughts were swirling around in my head. I realized that I needed to choose who it was that I was recovering for – because the only person that my choice truly affected was me. Furthermore, as I looked around at a room full of people without eating disorders, I couldn't help but smile. Every meal that I dreaded gave them delight, and every snack that left me shaking with fear only caused them to salivate. It was ironic, really, and quite healing... once I was able to broaden the scope of my vision enough that I could see it. I, the theoretically sane one, was spending most of my days dwelling on something as insignificant as a muffin, amidst a community of sociologically labeled "crazy" folk whose daily delight was dessert. Perspective is a bitch.

I ended up spending a total of eight days in that ward, although my first 48 hours of captivity remain nothing more than a drug-induced blur thanks to the doctor's attempt to pacify my panic attacks with various prescriptions. Slowly but surely, however, I began to gain back a shred of cognition and composure, and – given there was not much to do during those days other than eat, think about eating, sit and then eat again – I began to take time to make amends with my mind and body. And so, I started to savor my time alone meditating in the courtyard as an opportunity to pause, breathe and practice *feeling* my feelings.

I am hungry, my stomach would grumble, as I gently stretched my arms toward the sky.

Huh? What's that feeling? Hunger? I was confused. *Am I supposed to feel hungry? I just ate. How can I be hungry?*

I am tired, my drooping eyes exclaimed as the anxiety that had awoken me at dawn every morning began to ease.

Fatigue? What do I do with that? Am I allowed to nap? Should I push through it? How will I sleep at night if I rest during the day? Again, I was confused.

I am broken, my body screamed as my limbs grew increasingly stiff and sore with every passing day.

Why am I feeling worse if I'm resting? I haven't worked out in days... am I ever going to feel healthy again?

It was quite fascinating to begin to feel again, but it was also fear-inducing. I felt, but I didn't trust my feelings of hunger or fullness, nor did I know how to respond to them. I was eating, and eating a lot, but I came to find that I was actually losing weight because my body was working tirelessly to restore itself after years of intense exercise and restriction. I was resting but feeling more fatigued.

"Your lab work is improving much faster than expected," my doctor reported one day after lunch. "Your blood sugar levels seem to be balancing out, and your vitamin and mineral levels are looking good. You're lucky, you know. A lot of people don't bounce back." He paused to make sure he had my attention. "At this rate, we should be able to move you to residential care in a few more days."

"Great!" I exclaimed, but then I paused to reconsider. It wasn't *great*. True, a part of me wanted to leave, but it was safe in the hospital, and I wasn't sure that I was ready to face the real world on my own. I wanted to return to my life, but I knew that I hadn't been happy with the way I'd been living. I wanted to ditch the pre-planned microwave dinner diet of the unit – and stop further constipating my already clogged intestines – but I knew that that I couldn't be trusted to pick or portion my own meals. (Note that the anorexic excretory system usually doesn't respond to inpatient care as well as the rest of the body does.) I wanted my freedom back, but I knew that the disordered life that awaited me beyond the unit's walls was a far cry from free.

"Maybe in a few days," I finally responded. True, I needed something other than a box of crayons to keep me from going insane in that asylum, but I did not yet know what the next step was – nor if I was ready for it.

One of the biggest challenges for me in both the hospital and residential settings was that neither facility allowed me to know my weight. I was being force-fed every day, but blinded to my body's response to food, and the secrecy made me feel as though I was not a part of my own recovery. As a result, I became increasingly fearful of numbers that I didn't know. My body felt stiff, sore and bloated all the time. I felt like I had gained 50 pounds during those initial days of intensive hospitalization, but I still wasn't very good at feeling.

"I saw my weight this morning, Doc," I admitted during our daily check-in.

A new nurse had awoken me that morning, and being unfamiliar with the eating disorder protocol, she had neglected to cover up the screen on the scale during weigh-ins.

"Well, you had to see it at some point," said my doctor nonchalantly. "What did you think?"

"I'm losing weight. How is that possible?" I'd been shocked just hours earlier to see that I was actually shrinking. Shocked – but simultaneously soothed knowing that I wasn't spiraling uncontrollably toward a new profession as a sumo wrestler.

"Your body was starving to the point that it had begun shutting down to conserve energy. Now that it is getting the nutrition and rest it needs to start the restoration process, it is having to work harder than it ever has before to rebuild."

"But my stomach is sticking out, and I feel disgusting and bloated all the time."

"Ha!" He laughed as he pointed at his charts. "That's to be expected given that you haven't pooped yet this week!" Though it was reassuring to see that he wasn't too worried about my condition, a week's worth of constipation had corrupted my sense of humor, so I struggled to laugh along with him. "Your body is trying to figure out how to function again, Ryan. You've beaten it up badly, so you are going to have to be patient while it learns to trust you again."

That conversation provided just the encouragement that I needed to pick up the unit's 80s-era wall-mounted phone that afternoon and dial the number of a residential program I'd been pondering in the nearby city of Half Moon Bay. I had been on the fence for days about adding another round of treatment, given how horrible I felt after the first week of it, but I also knew the alternative would not likely work in my favor. At the time, Ed was quite insistent that I get back to work and re-enter the world as quickly as possible; however, the reality was that I hadn't been present in the world for some time leading up to that point. Thus, a few more weeks wasn't likely going to stop it from spinning.

I knew that there was no way I would be able to mimic my hospital-prescribed diet on my own, and the push-ups I'd been sneaking when no one was looking had provided proof that I wasn't likely to stay still when freed from the staff's supervision, either. I knew that I was going to need a lot of support to rest and restore my body, mind and spirit in the weeks to come, but I also knew that I was lonely and bored in the psych center and in need of a more stimulating community. My life out in the real world had been full of people, and although my social life was most often restricted by Ed, at least I had consistent interaction with like-minded peers. The psych unit, on the other hand, may have had an abundance of activity, but I never felt a part of it. I wanted companionship. I wanted to sit at the dinner table alongside others who shared my struggles – not alone under the watchful eye of a nurse who was timing my every chew. I wanted to be able to exclaim, "Me too!" when someone spoke of their omelet-induced anxiety at breakfast or shared their struggle with the scale before sitting down for snack. I simply wanted a friend, someone whose feelings and fears I could relate to my own.

"You know, Ryan, I don't think you have an eating disorder." My psychiatrist's comment during our final meeting before my discharge caught me off guard.

"Oh really? Well, in that case, I guess I'm wasting a lot of time and money by being here." A tinge of affirmation-seeking sarcasm reverberated in my reply.

"I don't think you have an eating disorder. I think that you are lonely and struggling with a lack of intimacy." She paused. "A lack that you have learned how to numb with food and exercise throughout the 30 years following your father's cancer diagnosis. However, the fact that you are here shows that food and exercise are no longer fulfilling."

"I tried the dating thing a few times," I said, pausing to allow the blooper reel that was my love life to stream through my mind. "It didn't work out too well," I finally concluded. "That's okay, though. My disorder started before puberty, so, given that I never experienced a non-anorexic attraction to girls, I guess I don't know what I am missing out on." Let me not fail to mention that, at this point, my psychiatrist was actually a very attractive woman who was roughly my age and did not appear to have a wedding ring on her finger.

"I'm not talking about dating, Ryan. I'm talking about intimacy. Intimacy and acceptance. Intimacy with those who love you – all those people in your life that you have been pushing away – and acceptance. Acceptance of who you are, apart from your eating and exercise habits."

Damn, if she wasn't right. I've always been a people person – outwardly, at least – meaning I'm overly charismatic and quick to make friends... or, should I say, acquaintances. To an outsider, it would seem that I was anything but lonely, and had I been able to invite any of those acquaintances into my secret life, that observation might have been true. Unfortunately, the only intimate relationship I could truly claim was the one I shared with Ed. So, in that sense, my psychiatrist was correct: I didn't have an eating disorder because an eating disorder is only a symptom of a larger lack in our lives. That was unfortunate because printing out a meal plan to address my nutritional deficiencies seems a much simpler solution than seeking out the reason why I wanted to starve myself.

"You're going to figure this out, Ryan." She smiled. "When you do, you are going to help a lot of people."

"I hope you're right, Doc, but it sure doesn't feel that way."

"That's why you're moving on to residential care." She put her hand on mine... and I melted. (Hey – can you really blame me? A lot of people develop crushes on their shrinks.) "No one expects you to overcome this on your own."

That was the last conversation that I shared with my psychiatrist, and I made a pact with myself upon leaving the hospital that I would mail her a copy of this book after I completed it. It is a promise that has kept me from hitting the delete button many a morning when the disorder has felt too daunting or the depression too real. It was an agreement that I made because, though I didn't yet feel worthy enough to get well for me, I was willing to fight through the recovery fatigue for others.

CHAPTER 19

ROLLING INTO RESIDENTIAL

Despite my not-so-celebratory spirit, the final 48 hours of my eight-day hospital stay happened to fall on Fourth of July weekend, which meant that a skeleton crew kept the hospital running while the rest of the world revved up to party and play. As a result, all purposeful programming was put on pause, and visits from the occupational therapists, chaplains and psychiatrists were replaced by mind-numbing movie marathons and puzzles (often with missing pieces). Furthermore, the nutritionist had also snuck away on vacation. So, as if our meals weren't sad enough before, they were now served with the peel-off plastic wrap still covering them! It was frustrating. I'd worked so hard throughout the course of the previous week to overcome the paralyzing panic and self-pity I'd felt when I'd entered the ICU; however, an all-too-familiar feeling of victimization – like the one brought on by that damn Otis Spunkmeyer muffin – had returned. I didn't want to watch movies. I didn't want to eat microwave dinners. I didn't want to engage in idle chit-chat with other patients, and I no longer wanted to be locked up in a sterilized hospital prison. I had lost any sense of gratitude for where I was or for the help that I was getting, and I simply wanted to go home, despite knowing just how dangerous a desire that was. I was losing motivation with each passing moment – and that was really scary.

"Yes, we actually do have a bed available," the voice on the other end of the line said. "It just opened up this morning."

"Really!?" I just about jumped out of my hospital gown! Somehow, by the grace of God (or Krishna, perhaps), I had managed to get a hold of the intake coordinator at the residential house in Half Moon Bay that I had been hoping to enroll in the following week. And not only was there an open bed, but there was a chance that I might be able to move in early!

"We have a bed, but unfortunately, we don't usually do admissions on the weekends." My heart broke. "It would be better to wait until the doctor gets back on Tuesday."

"I don't think I can last here in the hospital until Tuesday." I was desperate. It was Saturday at the time, and, though I wasn't sure where I was going, I had already asked the nursing staff to prepare my discharge paperwork. I was either heading home or entering into residential treatment – just another of my absurdly inflexible, self-imposed "either/or" anorexic conclusions. If there is one thing of which I have grown aware on the random days that I am sane enough for self-observation, it is that those of us who are afflicted with anxiety and/or eating disorders seem to live our lives with an obnoxiously impatient sense of urgency. Every decision is life or death. Every action is all or nothing. This false sense of urgency, coupled with an inability to look beyond the present moment, has repeatedly barred me from being present enough to enjoy what's right in front of me or make a logical life decision. At the time, I was safely situated in a hospital setting, one into which I had begged to be admitted for over a month, but I (or Ed) had made the decision that I needed to leave. Like, that day, right then. Why? Because, in my malnourished mind, the world was going to end when snack was served if I did not have plan in place for an afternoon escape.

"Well, it is not ideal, but since we already have your referral on file, I might be able to pull some strings and get you in." My broken heart started beating again. There was hope! "If you can get here before 2pm today," she added.

Fast-forward a few hours, and I was on my way to a quaint residential home in Half Moon Bay, California, in preparation for the third leg of my crazy treatment journey – and the hour-long Uber ride that separated the hospital from that house presented a perfect opportunity for reflection. I was able to sit back, close my eyes and daydream about my adventure thus far, while re-living the lessons I'd learned through my interactions with a diverse group of sociologically stigmatized, kind of kooky people.

It was a peaceful and pleasantly uneventful drive through the hills and along the coast on that Sunday afternoon – that is, until an all-too-familiar road sign wreaked havoc on my restfulness. I can still feel the flood of indecisiveness that met me as we passed by the Santa Cruz exit...

Am I making the right decision? Should I go home and return to life as it was or keep quiet and give residential treatment a go? Do I have the energy to keep going in recovery? I wasn't sure, but I did know that I didn't have the energy to continue living life without it.

It was in that moment, as we sped by my last exit opportunity, that one final question silenced all the others: *Do I have the desire to keep on living?*

Luckily, I knew that I didn't have the guts or the inclination to go for the alternative, so, with the big green sign for Santa Cruz fading away, I brushed aside any thoughts of a slow, starvation-induced suicide and pushed forward in the hope that I would soon regain the ability to look at myself in a mirror.

Before I knew it, we had made our way 70 miles up the coast to my new home away from home, a quiet, little property nestled in the rolling, flower-lined hills of Northern California. At first glance, I couldn't help but wonder if I was entering into residential care or going on a retreat; but regardless, the warm welcome that I received from three happy-go-lucky goats offered reassurance that I'd made the right decision. Tucked behind the goat pen, a small garden was in bloom, which provided fresh fruits and vegetables to the kitchen. It all seemed too good to be true, and for the first time in quite some time, I was overcome by a rather odd feeling: peace. Sadly, peacefulness is all too often a passing emotion – and, while the gardens surrounding my new home were a welcome contrast to the cold concrete hospital courtyard, I quickly came to realize that, though rest and relaxation are important components of the restoration process, recovery is certainly no retreat!

I barely had time to take a breath of the salty sea breeze or return the smiles from a trio of new housemates crocheting on the patio before being pulled away by the intake coordinator to go over the house rules and complete some paperwork. And, sweet mother of Mary, there were a lot of rules and even more paperwork! We finished filling out forms just as I was beginning to lose feeling in my right hand and, having half an hour to spare before supper, we set off on a brief tour of the property. There were chickens and rabbits to play with, and there was an inviting hiking trail to *look* at, since hiking, walking and excessive standing were strictly forbidden. We passed by a half-acre garden from which to pick salad toppings, and a picturesque window that overlooked it – perfectly placed to soak in the sun as it set over the Pacific. I took a deep breath and, although my anxiety had spiked just a few moments earlier while signing away my life, I once again felt at peace. I had made the right decision. And what's more, upon re-entering the house, I didn't dread the microwave-free meal that was being prepared in the kitchen!

"Ryan, it is so great to have you here." The nutritionist greeted me with excitement as she opened a binder with each resident's nutritional needs neatly graphed out on its pages. Before I could echo her salutation, she ambushed me with a barrage of questions. "What are your favorite foods? What don't you like? Is there a challenge food you'd like to try?"

"Um. Well, I…" The array of foods in the kitchen suddenly overwhelmed me, and I felt my heart rate escalate as my eyes drifted across the counter. It was too much to take in. I hadn't realized it at the time, but being stripped of choice in the hospital had eased my fear of making choices to the point that I was unable to decide on my own dinner! I was overcome by the surplus on the shelves and the nutritionist's questions, so I didn't answer her – I just stared at the counter in a state of stupefied silence.

"Don't worry about it for now," she said, sensing my increasing anxiety. "We will meet tomorrow and work together to create a meal plan. For now, all you have to do is decide between chicken or fish, broccoli or salad, a potato or a roll, and which two condiments you'd like to complement it all."

Hmm… I actually liked all those things. Moreover, I was hungry! Or, should I say, I was allowing myself to feel hunger.

"How about fish, a potato with sour cream, and a salad with vinaigrette dressing." I breathed sigh of relief upon getting my order out.

"Great! You can go ahead and prepare your plate."

"Prepare my plate?!" That fleeting feeling of peacefulness flipped to panic! It'd been hard enough to decide what I wanted to eat. Now I had to portion each item while a pair of eyes peered down at my plate? Ugh!

"Hmm…" she muttered in response to my pitiful attempt at plating. "We are going to need you to cut that salad in half but double the dressing. Then, add a second fish fillet and a second scoop of sour cream to top off that potato."

I looked down at my dish with disappointment while painstakingly pouring salad dressing over an otherwise orthorexic-friendly field of greens. Maybe I didn't make the right decision after all. Maybe I should've had that Uber driver veer off at the Santa Cruz exit so that I could continue my in anorexic ways in isolation. This sudden rush of apprehensiveness quickly overshadowed my appetite, and I could feel my intestines tying themselves in knots as I tiptoed over to the dinner table.

***

This is a great opportunity to dive into brief discussion about the relationship that exists between our heads and our guts. For as far back as I can remember, I have never had a particularly praiseworthy digestive system. My first memories of my mood-affected gut come from Christmastime when I was a young child. Every year, in anticipation of the lights and presents, I would spend Christmas Eve in bed with a bellyache while my friends laughed and played in the snow outside. The excitement of Santa Claus was just a bit too intense and, as I've come accept, excitement is nothing more than a positive form of anxiety. In the years to follow those youthful Christmas cramps, doctors have diagnosed my digestive difficulties as leaky gut, gastritis, gastroparesis and IBS. While those are all very real diagnoses, the bottom line is that no matter what you name it, a tumultuous tummy is often initiated (and/or exasperated) by anxiety. I could go through a slew of the symptoms I've experienced, ranging from diarrhea to constipation to migraines to indigestion, but each of my ailments can be traced back to stress. And unfortunately, anxiety cannot be pacified by Pepto-Bismol. However, I have found that a few simple breathing exercises and a little mindful movement before a meal can make a huge difference in helping me feel hunger cues and dodge any anxiety-induced indigestion. So, while the mind-gut connection remains a bit of a chicken-and-egg conundrum in terms of which causes which, developing an understanding of the roots of our digestive difficulties might just be the best way to overcome the anxiety that causes them... or subdue any anxiety they cause! Now, back to supper.

***

By the time we finally sat down for dinner that evening, the chaos of the day had taken its toll and left me too exhausted to make friends with my new housemates, let alone enjoy the food that had been piled upon my plate. Thus, I proceeded to stare blankly at my meal and wait, impatiently, for an invitation to start eating in the hope that I could put the drama of dinner behind me and prepare for bed.

"Check-in time!" the counselor exclaimed in an annoyingly excited tone, drawing attention to the little laminated piece of paper that he handed to my tablemate. "What are you feeling this evening, Elise?"

The question caught me off guard even though it wasn't directed at me. I didn't know what I felt. All I knew was that I didn't like whatever it was that I was feeling – nor did I like knowing that his question was bound to circle around the table and eventually land on me.

"I feel hopeless and overwhelmed," the young blond seated to my right replied. It was hard to hear, but slightly healing at the same time. It was hard because I could tell by looking into her eyes that these were not new emotions, but healing because, upon hearing her honest reply, I was able to recognize both emotions in myself. She then passed the paper to me.

"Ryan, welcome to our home." The counselor redirected his gaze toward the circle of words that I'd been handed. "We like to start each meal with the feeling wheel. Take a minute to survey your emotions. Then, when you're ready, share with us what you are feeling this evening."

As I read the array of adjectives that encircled the wheel, I was able to feel each emotion its own unique way. Fearful. Grateful. Apathetic. Anxious… I resonated with them all. Thus, it was in that moment that I realized something sad. I'd spent most of my life fleeing from the feelings on the paper in front of me instead of allowing myself to actually feel them.

"I feel confused!" I paused, and I could feel my anxiety slowly evolve into acceptance. "Confused… but also encouraged, because I finally feel like I am where I am supposed to be." I wasted no time in passing the wheel off to the middle-aged woman seated to my left so that the pre-meal ritual could continue. The experience had been slightly awkward, but I had to admit, it did feel good to voice my feelings. Moreover, I felt grateful for the wheel because I still had a long way to go until I could figure out what I felt without having a list of adjectives in front of me.

"Good job, gang," the counselor said approvingly as the last of my eight housemates shared with the group. "You now have 30 minutes to finish your dinner. You may begin."

"Who's up for a game?" someone asked from across the table before I had a chance to put a fork to my fish.

"I vote for 20 questions," a college-aged girl called out from deep within the shadows of the oversized sweatshirt that seemed to have swallowed her.

It seemed slightly ironic, really. We would begin each meal by sharing our feelings, only then to distract ourselves from feeling them anymore by playing tacky trivia games. Furthermore, as I found upon getting the first of my 20 questions "yellow-carded," not only were we expected to disregard our feelings once the meal had commenced, but we were also not allowed to mention anything related to food, exercise, religion, politics, clothing size or any other possible trigger topic that would naturally arise during an average dinner time discussion.

It didn't take many more yellow cards for me to accept that the safest approach to suppertime was to mute myself and focus on the unspoken feelings I had about the food in front of me, instead of the discussion taking place around me. Oh, and let me not fail to mention that eating also came with its own set of restrictions! We were not to mix our food, cut it too small, consume pieces that were too large, chew excessively, eat too slowly, swallow too quickly, drink too much water, etc., etc., etc. All said and done, it'd be safe to say that we like rules in residential treatment – and, unfortunately, the program's obsessive adherence to them was not very helpful for overcoming the compulsions that I had already imposed on my own eating practices. Thus, whereas I had entered residential care with high hopes of finding freedom with food, I left less than a week later with an elevated obsession about it. That said, I want to be careful not to discourage any of you that may be on the fence about residential treatment because even my abbreviated attempt was essential in the restoration of my sanity, weight and self-worth. Just don't make the same mistake that I made and run away when the reality of recovery rears its head.

Throughout both of my residential experiences, art proved to be a powerful tool in allowing me to explore and express my many emotions on and beyond that goofy feeling wheel – emotions that I couldn't otherwise comprehend. With that in mind, I encourage you to think of residential treatment as a blank canvas. From the time that I left Shepard Pratt's program at age 19, to my dive back into care in Half Moon Bay at age 36, I'd been painting a proverbial portrait of what I thought recovery should look like. It had started off well; however, if any of you are aspiring artists, then you might be familiar with the concept of overworking a painting. Every time that I didn't like a metaphorical brush stroke, I would simply splatter more paint on top of it in a haphazard attempt at covering it up instead of stepping back and assessing how to best incorporate it into the picture. When we approach perceived mistakes – and I stress the word "perceived" – by adding more paint, once-distinct colors start to blur into a brownish mishmash. Clouds turn chaotic and waves turn to whitewash. The more paint we add, the further we get from the picture we had in mind. We begin to lose patience. This is the way of the world. Life outside of treatment can be a mess of colors and brushstrokes – and as much as we all love abstract art, it is important to acknowledge that nothing of artistic excellence comes from panicked painting. Residential care is unique in that it provides us with a clear canvas on which to make a fresh start, and it allows us to pause alongside a supportive team so that we may figure out what it is we hope to create before ever putting paint to paper – that is, if we give it the chance.

So, is residential treatment a necessity? No. However, it sure can make things a whole lot easier! So, if you feel that your life has gotten a little out of control, consider making the process a little less painful on yourself by enrolling in a supportive program.

Are you likely to leave residential treatment with a Rousseau-approved recovery masterpiece? Ha! Far from it! As the earlier table-talk example illustrated, life in treatment is sheltered, to say the least. The real world is going to meet you with triggers and tribulations for which no residential stay can fully prepare you. Expect it! However, if you take the time during residential treatment to paint the backdrop for your recovery panorama, then you may find the that the sheltered environment has equipped you with the skills necessary to turn real-world curveballs into the finishing touches of your recovery masterpiece. You see, we are each uniquely responsible for painting the life that we want to live. On occasion, that might mean we need to clear the canvas, but no matter what, always remember that it is perfectly possible to be both a work in progress AND an example of artistic excellence simultaneously.

CHAPTER 20

REFLECTIONS ON RESIDENTIAL CARE

I don't want to focus too much on the residential side of recovery in this book because it is important that you make your own decisions about it and have your own experiences with it. What I would like to touch upon instead are a few of the barriers that block us from receiving the gift of residential care. The biggest of these blockades came up in a conversation I had one afternoon with the Half Moon Bay house's nutritionist.

"You have been here for three days now, Ryan. How are things going?"

"Okay, I guess." I had entered our dialogue that day with an agenda – a common occurrence for a slightly obsessive, absurdly compulsive, type-A anorexic. So, I answered her question apathetically while awaiting an opportunity to dive into my pre-planned discourse.

"Just okay?"

"Yep. Just okay." This was my shot – my time to speak up, state my case and change the program that they had me on. So, I took it. "I have to admit that I am getting a little bored these days and... well... I really don't love the six-meal-a-day re-feeding routine you have me on." I paused to see if she wanted to chime in, but her shiftless gaze told me to continue. "I guess, what I am trying to say is that... well... I was hoping you would work with me to figure out what it looks like to live normally, like I would in the real world, and not just stuff me full of snacks and shakes."

Silence.

"I feel like I am gaining weight too quickly, like I am eating much more than I could or would ever eat on my own. The whole thing feels a bit uncomfortable, not to mention unsustainable."

"I see. So, what do you propose we do?"

"Well, we could change up my meal plan a bit? Cut out a snack during the day so that I'm hungrier at dinner? And maybe you could let me start breakfast a little earlier than 8am?" They seemed like reasonable suggestions to me. After all, we were woken up at 6am, my meals were already much larger than those of the other residents, and I would never eat six times a day on my own. "Oh yeah," I said, gaining a little more confidence, "maybe we could add in a little exercise as well? Nothing crazy. Just a couple of short walks and a little yoga a few times a day to loosen up my body." I paused before blurting out, "And my excretory system!"

"Well, Ryan, you are gaining weight; however, that is one of your main goals in being here. And no one expects you to maintain the same diet in the 'real world' that you are on here. That's good because you aren't going to be re-feeding for the rest of your life. This is simply one phase of the process – and an essential, albeit difficult one. For the time being, what do you say you kick back and allow us to help you get back to health?" She sent a wink my way. "Maybe it would be helpful, in that regard, to stop thinking about this phase of treatment as 're-feeding.' What do you say we call it 'body rejuvenation' instead?"

I had grown all too accustomed to the term "re-feeding" during the hospitalization phase of treatment, despite despising the sound of it; thus, her suggested change of wording was quite appealing.

"One of the most common reasons our residents report as a reason for avoiding residential treatment lies in the re-feeding model that is often associated with it. That is to be expected! A six-meal-a-day, dessert-inclusive diet would be intimidating for anyone, but for an anorexic coming out of a period of prolonged restriction, it is outright paralyzing, not to mention uncomfortable – physically and psychologically! But that is why you are here, Ryan, because very few people can do it alone."

She put her hand on mine, and I nodded to let her know I was still paying attention.

"Your body is smarter than you give it credit for, you know. Unfortunately, given the many years of mixed-up messages that you've been sending it by restricting, binging and purging through exercise, it is going to take a little time before that body of yours begins to trust you again. For the time being, just expect that your metabolic system is going to be little erratic, and trust in the process. You've pushed your body to its limits. In turn, it's going to require a good bit of rest and a lot more fuel than it will need in the future. It also has gotten pretty used to being starved, so don't be surprised if it clings to those initial calories that you're putting in it out of fear it won't have enough to sustain itself later. Your weight will fluctuate a bit as it works to figure out what it is like to be fed. That is why we don't want you looking at the scale while you are here. Health is holistic, Ryan, and 'wellness' isn't defined or confined to a certain weight or calorie count."

"Don't let the rest of the house hear you say 'calorie' too loudly or you'll likely get yellow-carded," I said with a hint of sarcasm. "It's one of the program's 10,000 trigger words, you know!"

"Depending on your interpretation, I guess it is. However, after spending a semester in Mexico during graduate school, I came to appreciate the Spanish vantage point a little bit more than our American one."

"Does that mean that I should I expect tacos for dinner tonight?"

She laughed. "Tacos are certainly one of my favorite forms of calories; however, I was actually referring to the translation of the term itself into Mexican Spanish – not the foods from which they get them." She smiled upon revealing their word for calories: "*¡Energía!*" she exclaimed.

"Like… energy?"

"Precisely! You won't find many Mexicans obsessing over nutrition labels because they understand food in terms of *energy* output instead of *caloric* intake. Maybe that is why they seem so much happier on that side of the border." She smiled. "They have the *energy* to smile!"

The wisdom and re-wording she offered during that conversation not only helped to change my perspective on the re-feeding period of recovery, but it also paved the way for a simple science lesson as well.

As those who didn't doze off during chemistry class might remember, a calorie is nothing more than the energy required to raise one gram of water's temperature by one degree Celsius. "Calorie" doesn't mean weight gain. It doesn't relate to whether someone's skinny or fat. And, in the correct context, it really isn't a very scary word at all. In fact, given that one of the more obnoxiously common symptoms of an eating disorder is that we are constantly cold, calories – or energy that can be converted to heat – should be incredibly sought-after solutions! In a similar regard, the term "body rejuvenation" is a much more pleasant-sounding description of the restoration phase of recovery. Rejuvenation is about reviving our energy – and energy carries with it a connotation of joy and pleasure. So, if you are an ardent calorie counter or nutrition-label reader, how about pausing and scribbling "energía" over the word "calories" on the panic-inducing items in your pantry?

That nutritionist was quite wise in her assessment. The frustrating part came in hearing it! Since the day I was first rolled into the ICU, my body had been on a rejuvenation roller coaster – and a lack of nutritional consistency and rest would only prolong the already arduous rejuvenation process. If I would sit still and follow a meal plan for a while, I knew that my metabolism, mental well-being and weight would all self-regulate. Unfortunately, knowing isn't trusting – and I have never been able to trust my own body. As a result, my body has been unable to trust me. Thus, the rollercoaster ride continues, and a new term comes into play.

Flash-forward: "You're suffering from a pretty severe case of adrenal fatigue," declared my doctor upon listening to my heartbeat, my complaints and the long list of symptoms that I'd brought up during a physical a few weeks after my early exit from residential care.

"But… I've gained weight?"

It was alarming how alarming it was to hear myself mutter those words. Indeed, I had gained a few pounds; however, I had also fallen back into my habitual exercise cycle. Thus, knowing that my weight was still on the rise despite working out was worrisome. It was a strange feeling. I wanted to see my weight go up. I wanted to get stronger and feel healthier (or so I claimed). But when it did rise,

I panicked! I panicked because I was already living a much more active life and eating a fair amount healthier than most of my peers. Nevertheless, I was still getting heavier. I panicked because I wasn't feeling any healthier. In fact, I was feeling increasingly depleted. Finally, I panicked because, instead of feeling peaceful about the process, I was, well, feeling panicky!

Shouldn't my anxiety be going down as my weight goes up? How am I going to stop the weight gain once I reach a healthy weight? What is a healthy weight? Am I forever sentenced to a life of unsustainable exercise just to maintain a steady weight? Will I ever have a normal person's metabolic system?

I panicked because I knew that a life that revolved around daily gym visits and food restriction was not only unsustainable, but it was also unpleasant. I just wanted to be normal. To be able to rest without guilt, eat a normal meal without fearing that I'd spiral up to sumo-wrestler size, and focus my attention something other than food and/or movement for a change.

"Yes, your weight is up a *little;* however, it is still unhealthily low. As for why you are gaining weight despite exercising…" She paused. "The real question is, why are you exercising? Your body has gotten used to the unsustainable level of activity that you've been submitting it to, so, until you allow it to rest, any exercise you do will simply cause it to cling on to every calorie you put into it, and your metabolism will continue to slow down in response."

"I don't understand."

She rotated her laptop screen so that I could read along with her as she started reciting the list of symptoms attributed to adrenal fatigue syndrome. "Depression, anxiety, stress, insomnia, fatigue, hormonal and mood imbalance, low thyroid function and metabolic rates, weight fluctuation, confusion…" She looked up at me as I continued reading through the list of symptoms. "Need I continue?"

"Yeah, well…" The roster she read had pretty much parroted the issues that had brought me into her office that day.

"The good news is that the treatment for adrenal fatigue is really quite simple." A subtle smirk snuck across her lips before she added, "For the average American, that is!" Her smile exploded in a fit of laughter. "I need you to be lazy, Ryan!"

Just hearing the word evoked a feeling of self-disgust. "I don't know how to be lazy," I cried out. I was too anxious to sit still, and the thought of laziness only made me more anxious. I remembered the fatigued feeling that came with rest during my residential stay – and I feared its return. I had felt stiff and sore, with a bloated stomach that left me bouncing between anxiety and depression for a week straight. And with each day that I was deprived of my dopamine fix, I grew only more exhausted and irritable. Unfortunately, at that point, exercise wasn't proving a viable option either because, even though I had taken the liberty of re-introducing it into my recovery, I still felt like donkey dung while doing it – anxious, panicky, pathetic donkey dung!

"I hate to be the bearer of bad news, but it is going to take more than a week or two of rest in order restore your adrenal system. You are going to have to make a lifestyle change, and that isn't going to be easy. Once you do, however, I promise that your body will figure itself out. Just know that it is going to take some time. Moreover, even though your weight seems like it is bouncing up and down a lot right now, that is mostly just water retention. Have faith that, as your body continues to balance, so, too, will your weight and mood. For the time being, put your focus on your feelings instead of your physique and see if you can't improve the relationship that exists between your mind and body." She stood up and flipped her computer screen to sleep. "Check back in a month or so and let me know if you don't feel a little more balanced." With that, she walked out of the door, and I slowly followed suit.

***

A new word has been gaining popularity in the recovery world as of late… "interoception," defined as "one's personal perception of their body's internal functions (our heartbeat, hunger, breathing and nervous system) in relation to their emotions." Many health conditions (such as eating disorders, chronic pain, adrenal fatigue and addiction) are characterized by a lack of bodily awareness, or the feeling of "disembodiment," and awareness tools such as interoception can help us regain our natural rhythms so that we might work with our bodies, rather than against them, as they begin to heal themselves. This requires that we first learn to listen to our bodies. Unfortunately, as much as I'd love to share with you a simple method for doing so, I have yet to figure it out for myself. That said, I am finding that a mixture of meditation, mindfulness and art have been incredibly helpful in my own journey, so much so that I recently joined a local chapter of the Recovery Dharma program that is based in Buddhist principles and increasing in popularity around the country. Now, let's jump back to my time in residential care in Half Moon Bay.

***

"You are showing a lot of improvement after only a few days," the nurse exclaimed, as she un-velcroed the blood pressure cuff wrapped around my right arm. "Your mood seems to be improving, and your body is responding well to re-feeding." She smiled as she held up the purple children's cuff. "If you keep progressing at this rate, we might even eventually be able to use the adult blood pressure cuff someday."

"Funny…" For as positive as her words were, they were also concerning to hear. True, I had embarked on my treatment journey some 11 days before with an intention to get well; however, I feared what "wellness" meant. The truth was, I feared the unknown, and wellness was one of the worrisome question marks in my life.

Simply typing that seems slightly absurd, so I'd imagine that reading it is a bit bizarre as well. But I had spent two decades being sick, so, for as unpleasant as the symptoms might have been, feelings of weakness, hunger and fatigue were strangely comforting because they were familiar. In other words, as long as I was unhealthy, I was safe. I could seek shelter in treatment and hide under a veil of meekness. I could exhaust my emotions with exercise or starve them away through restriction. I could put off pursuing my greater purpose until tomorrow while going through the motions of masochistic mediocrity today. So, yes, for as strange as it sounds, there's a large part of me that wanted to stay sick.

Why? Because I'd forgotten who I was apart from the disorder, and I feared finding out! My eating disorder had become how I defined myself… and, while this may be fine and dandy for those who would rather dodge their destinies than dive into them, I believe there is a reason for our existence that extends far beyond our ailments, eating-related or otherwise. I was not ready to stop searching for my reason quite yet. In that light, I'd like to share an excerpt that I read one morning while deep within the confines of that residential casa, in hope that the wise words of the one and only Marianne Williamson may help us all open our eyes to the possibilities of tomorrow, today.

Our deepest fear is not that we are inadequate. Our deepest fear is that we are powerful beyond measure. It is our light, not our darkness, that most frightens us. We ask ourselves, "Who am I to be brilliant, gorgeous, talented, fabulous?" Actually, who are you not to be? You are a child of God. Your playing small does not serve the world. There is nothing enlightened about shrinking so that other people won't feel insecure around you. We are all meant to shine, as children do. We were born to make manifest the glory of God that is within us. It's not just in some of us; it's in everyone. And as we let our own light shine, we unconsciously give other people permission to do the same. As we are liberated from our own fear, our presence automatically liberates others.

Williamson, in her widely quoted inspirational text, wasn't the only one to bestow a little wisdom on me during those long days of forced feeding. I also found companionship in the house's three goofy goats and the coop of chickens! As the lone guy in a flock of female residents, I often found it difficult to relate to my housemates; however, I very much enjoyed the conversations that I shared with the livestock out back. It was healing to feed my new friends and watch how they functioned on intuition instead of intellect. I came to find joy and acceptance sitting alongside the goats and journaling – minus one unfortunate incident when good ol' Gruffy ate my pencil and paper – and I thoroughly enjoyed the time I spent with my non-judgmental yard-mates. However, I mention them not because of the friendships that we formed, but because of a metaphor they reinforced.

***

There is an old fable in which a good-hearted farmer finds an eagle with a broken wing. With the best of intentions, the farmer rescues the eagle and places it in a chicken coop without access to a mirror or interaction with fellow members of his predatory species. Over time, the eagle begins to grow quite comfortable in the coop – complacent even, as he pecks his days away alongside the other chickens.

That all changes when a visitor stops by the farm one afternoon and, upon seeing the eagle clucking away amidst a community of chickens, asks the farmer if he might borrow the bird for an experiment. Upon the farmer's approval, the visitor gently picks up the bird of prey and climbs up a ladder that leads to the roof of the barn. When he reaches the top of the ladder, he walks to the edge of the roof, places the bird on precipice and waits for him to soar off into the sunset. But the eagle simply stands at the edge of the roof and peers down at his friends still feeding below.

The visitor grows increasingly impatient with the eagle and eventually offers a little encouragement in the form of a nudge. But the eagle won't fly. He simply flails and flutters his way back down to the coop.

The man tries several more times, but the only thing that takes flight is his frustration. Then, just he has about given up all hope, he spots a second eagle soaring through the sky far off in the distance. The man quickly returns to the coop, grabs the chicken-brained bird of prey and climbs the ladder one final time. The duo waits atop the rooftop for a few moments until the other eagle comes close. Then, as the silhouette of the soaring bird passes between them and the sun, the man tosses the eagle off the rooftop and holds his breath in anticipation.

At first, the bird flails and flutters its way back down toward the coop. But just as the man is about to give up hope, the flailing eagle catches a glimpse of its kin and something magical happens: The eagle spreads his healed wings wide and begins to soar.

That eagle had overstayed his welcome in the coop, and as such, he had forgotten his true identity. He had forgotten how to fly. I, on the other hand, under-stayed my advised treatment protocol and, as a result, have been battling my brokenness alone and vulnerable on the ground ever since. The lesson here is: There is a time to heal and there is a time to fly, but unfortunately, there is not a set timeline to tell us precisely when to spread our wings. Instead, we must learn to trust those who have a heart to help us heal, as well as our own authentic voice (which will grow in clarity as we progress in healing).

I'm hesitant to use too many analogies because I don't want to make it sound like our disordered thinking is all in our head. That said, it is kind of implied in the term *disordered thinking*. Regardless of where our disorders come from, one thing's for certain: It is exceedingly difficult to get out of our head… and far too easy to stay sick. Painful? Yes. Unpleasant? Quite. But fulfilling? Never.

It took a lot for that eagle to soar. Without the stranger's encouragement, he would never have made it to the rooftop, and without a fly-by from his feathered friend, he simply would have returned to the comforts of the coop. It takes a lot for us to spread our wings, too, and much like that eagle, we must welcome any external support we can get while we build up our inner strength. I'll close out that fable for the time being and return to my own residential story, but not before restating one essential truth: Treatment in any form is meant to empower and equip us for flight. It should never clip our wings.

***

Unlike the high-walled concrete courtyard of the hospital, the retreat-style residential home was quite beautiful – too much so, actually! On our patio I would sit, feeling imprisoned as I watched the sun bouncing across the surface of an ocean that I could not play in. It was a metaphor of my disorder, really. I wanted so badly to be free to splash and surf in the sea, but I was not able to venture past the edge of our patio. I wanted to live a life free from disordered thoughts around food, but my soul couldn't escape caloric confinement. Every day at the house was the same. Breakfast. Group. Goat feeding. Snack. Sit. Lunch. Group. Snack. Sit. Dinner. Sit. Snack. Sleep. Repeat. It didn't take long before I grew bored, and, as has been true in my past, boredom became a hinderance to my health. Up until day five, I had been doing a decent job of distracting myself by fiddling around on the house's guitar, journaling and teaching myself the fine art of juggling – that was, until my balls were taken from me because tossing them into the air constituted exercise. (There is a fully intended pun hidden in that last sentence that illustrates my feelings of frustration, which incited an unfortunate change in motivation.) I grew resentful, and, in response, I began to go through the motions of recovery as a means of appeasing the staff rather than a means of healing myself. I was in trouble.

I have stressed it before and will likely do so again: Recovery only works when it is rooted in self-love and a personal desire to be well. As soon as you seek to recover for a reason beyond your own well-being, you've already started to slip. As a minister, I often relate back to a story from the Gospel of John, in which a disabled man is found lying by a healing lake.

"I have no one to help me into the water," the man pouts to Jesus. The man had been lying on the shoreline for 38 years by that point, hoping that someone would come along and help him into the healing waters.

What Jesus said in response is quite significant to our situations, as well as the disabled man's, regardless of your faith. Jesus did not offer to help the man into the water, nor did he wave a magic wand over the man's withered limbs. Instead, he asked, "Do you want to be made well?"

Let me repeat: Recovery only works when it is rooted in self-love and a desire to heal (not to *be healed*.) That doesn't mean that you must do it by yourself, but it does mean that you have to do it *for* yourself. It means that you must have faith in yourself. It means that you must want to be made well.

"Pick up your mat," Jesus then commanded. "Your faith has healed you."

Note the language used there: "*Your* faith has healed you." This is a power statement, and we like power statements in recovery! We have the power to heal ourselves… if (and that's a big "if") we have faith. That may mean having faith in a program that seems painful or purposeless. It may mean having faith in some supreme being who you know will never push you beyond your abilities… but who will indeed push you. It may mean having faith in a therapist who encourages you to step out of your comfort zone. It may mean having faith in a family member or friend to whom you can turn for help – and from whom you can accept help when it is offered. It may mean any number of things; however, none of them mean anything if you do not have faith in yourself and your own ability to be healthy.

I was called to have faith in the process, but for me, having faith in the process didn't mean putting the next foot forward. It meant staying put, which is exactly the opposite of what I proceeded to do.

"I think I am ready to try life again," I told the house psychiatrist on day six of my stay.

"I think you are too," she said, smiling. "But certainly not on your own."

"I haven't missed a meal, supplement or snack yet. I am feeling stronger." I had approached residential care as a quick reset. Now that my chronic panic attack had been pacified and my weight was on the upswing, I had begun to develop a false sense of confidence, a phantasmal belief that I could continue the path my own.

"Do you mind me asking why you're in such a rush to get back into the real world?"

I couldn't answer her. I was always in a rush. Whether I was walking my dog on a Saturday morning, standing in line at the supermarket or sitting through a work meeting, I always had my sights set on the next endeavor. Moreover, my rushed approach to life had only gotten worse over the past several years. My jaw was always clenched, my stomach was always tight, my breath was always short, and my stare was always stern.

"It's not that I am in a rush…" I said in my own defense (despite knowing every word I spoke was untrue). "I just think that I've gotten what I needed to get from residential."

"Well then, congratulations! I am pretty sure that your five-day stay sets the record for the fastest recovery ever recorded." Her sarcasm was unappreciated, but appropriate.

"Very funny. Does that mean that you will sign off on my referral for outpatient treatment?"

"Not a chance!" She smiled once again, though her dimples quickly disappeared this time around. "We haven't even scratched the surface of what brought you here, Ryan. You don't just have an eating disorder. You have a deficiency in your life that you mask with food and exercise, a void that cannot be filled by an additional snack or supplement. Not to mention, I highly doubt you will continue with snacks or supplements the second that you step out the door."

Her words echoed those of the hospital's psychiatrist just one week before, and with them I was whisked away into a flashback from my youth. It'd been nearly 30 years since I started acting on strange impulses and isolating myself through food and exercise, so I couldn't deny that she was right. My eating and exercise obsessions were rooted in something much more significant than the numbers on a scale.

"Eating disorders are tricky things," she said after several seconds of silence. "Even if you were able to maintain the diet that we've gotten you started on, I would be hesitant to think that you could uncover the roots of your disorder on your own. And, honestly, I am not too sure that is a road you'd really want to travel alone." A look of deep concern spread across her face. "The world doesn't just want to see you physically healthy, Ryan. It wants to see you happy. It's not about weight. You've proven over the years that you can dance that dance – despite this recent near fatal slip-up, that is. It's about self-acceptance. Acceptance of yourself, regardless of waistlines or lunchtimes."

She was right, but unfortunately, she was too late. I had already decided that I was moving on. I was rushed without reason. I had been given a gift – an opportunity to untangle the emotions behind my exercise addiction and disordered eating in a safe and secure environment, but I'd grown restless in, and resistant to, the residential care that I had begged to enter for more than a month. I was no longer present in that house on the shores of Half Moon Bay because I had lost faith in my ability to heal and my motivation to try. I was solely there to appease others, and all my actions to follow were attempts to trick the team into setting me free.

It was Friday evening when I walked out of her office, and the house was preparing for their weekly pizza party. I use the term "party" gently because all its attendees ended up being party poopers. So much anxiety filled the air as we filled our plates with cheesy, triangular tools of torture that any observer would have thought that the pizza was poisoned. When the feeling wheel was passed around that evening, each emotion was in some way somber or scared. "Hopeless." "Fearful." "Disgusted." Our party was dismal, to say the least – and that only drove my desire for an early discharge.

I managed to tough out dinner that evening, but my disdain, coupled with an excessive amount of dairy, proved hard to digest, and that left me physically and psychologically constipated the next morning. Just two weeks prior, I'd yearned for nothing more than the safe sanctuary of a residential program; however, once I was there, I found myself feeling like I was imprisoned. I'd somehow forgotten the panic and pain I felt leading up to treatment. I'd forgotten how lonely I had felt as I cut through the fog in my kayak with nothing more than a breadcrumb in my stomach for sustenance. I couldn't remember why I had entered treatment because I had made up my mind – which was still notably malnourished – to leave against medical authority the next day. And that is exactly what I did.

After skimping on breakfast that morning and skipping snack, I marched boldly into the nurse's office with discharge forms in hand. I knew that my escape would be easier on the weekend when the medical staff wasn't around to plead their case, but what I did not know was that leaving would burn a bridge with my insurance company, thus barring me from receiving any outpatient care afterwards. So, yes, I was free, but I was far from ready to fly. I was an eagle, tossed from a residential rooftop, with a broken wing that had yet to heal.

CHAPTER 21

WHAT IS "RECOVERY" OR "BEING RECOVERED"?

Alice asked of the Cheshire Cat who was sitting in a tree,
"What road do I take?"
The curious, kind of crazy, cat responded with a question of
his own. "Well, where do you want to go?"
"I don't know," Alice answered.
"Then it really doesn't matter which road you take to get
there, does it?"

              – Lewis Carroll, *The Adventures of Alice and Wonderland*

I left residential care that afternoon with a determined spirit, raring to travel recovery road on my own. The only problem was, I didn't know where it was that I was trying to go. With that in mind, I figured this would be a great time to break from my story and explore a question that will guide your own: What the hell is "recovery?"

How many nights have I laid awake, staring at the darkened ceiling, dreading another indecisive early-morning encounter at the crossroads of recovery? That "road" metaphor everyone loves to use to depict recovery is great if we know where it is we are hoping to get to… but damn, if my road thus far hasn't been filled with forks! These metaphorical forks have made me second guess my direction every time I am faced with a difficult decision. And then there are the literal forks that stab at my soul every time I use them to consume something out of my comfort zone, such as a syrup-soaked sausage link or a scrambled egg.

If you are at all like me, then you might agree that indecisiveness is the root of most of our inner turmoil and eating disorder angst. So, what do you say we address a bit of that indecisiveness-induced anxiety by attempting to discern where it is that we are heading? In other words, how about we reword Alice's question from the excerpt at the start of the chapter to answer a quintessential query: What exactly is recovery, and what road will lead us there?

Though our answers to that question will vary, my personal response reflects a trifecta of diagnoses that have plagued me over the years – three disordered legs of one unbalanced stool, each one perpetuating the other two in an unfortunate, antagonistic way. Throughout the recovery process, I've joked that I could tackle any two of those three ED traits at any given time, if only the third would stop taunting me from the sidelines; however, unfair as it seems, we don't get to pick our impediments.

What is my cocktail of kookiness? Well, if you haven't picked up on it by this point, I have long been plagued by a rather ridiculous balance – or absurd imbalance – of exercise bulimia and anorexia, with a side of obsessive compulsive disorder (OCD). Though I am not sure which of the troublesome trio came first, they now work together to create a vicious cycle in which my exercise bulimia pushes me to sweat, swim or stretch off the excess calories that I *thought about* eating, but that my anorexia led me to restrict, while my obsessive compulsivity pushes me to eat less and move more each day to follow. Sadly, all that exercise-enhanced anorexic restrictiveness leads to a nightly binge that leaves me feeling guilty (and in gastrointestinal turmoil) the next morning. Thus, I awaken a bit ill but compelled to one-up the previous day's workout... and fuel it with fewer calories. Lo and behold, another day of starvation ends with another nighttime binge, which spurs another sleepless night and compels me to engage in another compulsive morning of exercise and restriction. I repeat this over and over and over again... until the vicious cycle lands me in the ICU with a pulse rate that sets off every alarm in the room. Ugh! What was it that Einstein said about insanity? It is characterized by repeating the same mistakes but expecting different results. Of course, many state that Einstein himself was about as kooky as our friend, the Cheshire Cat; however, "crazy" is simply how society likes to label people they later describe as geniuses.

Now that you're a little more in tune with my idiosyncrasies, let me invite you along for a quick flashback into the psych-unit stint of my treatment, so you can better understand the essence of this so-called recovery toward which we are all wandering. I didn't have much to do during those eight days I spent alongside a box of dull crayons in that asylum, other than contemplate the Cheshire Cat's question, "Where do you want to go?"

I wondered to myself, *If recovery is indeed a road, then where is it that I'm heading? Does "being recovered" mean maintaining a healthy weight without worrying about the fried wontons that snuck onto my dinner plate? If so, what is a "healthy weight," and what happens if I simply don't want wontons? Does "being recovered" mean making amends with a disorder that has defined my life for decades? If so, who am I without it, and how do I go about distancing myself from it? Does "being recovered" mean I can no longer go the gym or run on the beach at sunset? If so, what do I do without my depression-dulling dopamine fix? In other words, what the hell does everyone mean when they keep referring to "recovery," what road will lead me there, and is it even a place I want to travel to?*

It was during that time of confinement and contemplation that I started to study the other patients, doctors and nurses on the unit. In doing so, I started to see just how different each of their lives were. I also saw that none of the lives I was watching stood out as particularly appealing to me. My fellow psych patients spent their days drugged and dazed, watching reruns of old 90s sitcoms while acting on compulsions of their own. The nursing staff did not seem all too happy or healthy either, given that they spent most of their afternoons complaining about aching joints, juggled schedules, and the world that was awaiting them on the other side of the courtyard's walls. As for the doctors? No jealousy there! They had long since surrendered the twinkles in their eyes to the stress-induced wrinkles of overtime. So, while it was true that I was not in the healthiest of headspaces at the time, even in my emaciated state of being, I found my perception of health to be much different than the experts'.

"But I don't want to go among mad people," Alice remarked.
"Oh, you can't help that," said the Cat. "We're all mad here."

Yes! There it is… The secret to self-acceptance from the Cheshire
Cat himself: We should never feel alone in our kookiness because we
are *all* kooky characters. We are all *mad!* (Note that we have negated
the word "crazy" because, as the Cat put it, "I am not crazy. My
reality is simply different than yours.") Yes, we are all disordered in
some form or fashion – AND THAT IS OKAY, because recovery
is not the absence of kookiness, so much as it is a place where our
kookiness does not control us. Thus, maybe a better question to
ask ourselves while working toward recovery would be, *How can we
embrace our kookiness in a way that helps us create a life we want to live?*

That question may sound strange, but the more I pondered it,
the more relevant it became to my situation. *Maybe my dueling disorders
aren't all that detrimental,* I thought. After all, during those times when
my compulsivity is a little less obsessive, and my eating a little less
disordered, my personality peculiarities do keep me on schedule and
my house uncluttered. Hell, in the past, I've been known to knock
out eight hours of work in the gap between my 5:59am breakfast and
12:35pm lunch. True, it'd be nice to be a little more flexible, but when
the world doesn't inhibit my schedule, and malnourishment doesn't
mess with my mind, there are attributes of my illnesses that provide a
lighter lining to my mental illness clouds!

As for exercise? When done in moderation, it too has its benefits.
My love of yoga keeps me limber, and posing away my evenings
outdoors with a slightly elevated heart rate remains the best
prescription I've found for depression. Unfortunately, my adoration of
exercise became an addiction, and my once healthily elevatable heart
rate had slowed down to the point of orthostasis, but, heck, everyone
goes a little overboard on occasion… right? (By the way, orthostasis,
for those unfamiliar with the condition, is a common consequence
of starvation in which one's blood pressure drops to dangerous levels
upon standing. This can result in several unfortunate side effects, such
as dizziness, confusion, disorientation and, oh yeah, death.)

Finally, my ritualistic eating habits make me much more mindful than most as I savor every spoonful of cereal. Of course, mindful eating is only beneficial when one actually eats! All said, I obviously had some work to do if I ever hoped to put my restrictive eating habits, extreme exercise inclinations and compulsive character traits into the positive category; however, it's important to remember that there is, at least, a light at the end of the tunnel!

So, what does this all mean?

It means that there are attributes of my tri-diagnosis that could add value to my life and even aid in recovery – if I can figure out how to keep them from taking my life from me first! Thus, my personal understanding of recovery is not a life absent of any eating disorder symptoms or disordered behaviors, but a balanced life in which Ed is a distant acquaintance… not a spouse. Recovery means taking the *disordered* out of my eating, the *obsessive* out of my doings, and the *addiction* out of my exercise. It doesn't mean abstinence as it might with a drug addiction – one cannot abstain from food or movement. It means balance, awareness and acceptance. We must have awareness that some of our symptoms are simply a part of our personalities, and we must accept that we are all a little disordered – and that our disorders do not define us.

There are many who might oppose this relational view of recovery, and for most addictions, I would agree with them. For the heroin addict or alcoholic, abstinence is essential; however, what makes an eating disorder so damn difficult is that abstinence is not an option. So, while many might believe that you can, and should, completely obliterate all compulsive behaviors around exercise and eating, I don't think this is true, nor always fully possible. Instead, recovery, for me, is a space where I am free to choose what I do or eat in response to what my body is craving, rather than on what my compulsive habits are coaxing me to do and/or consume. Recovery means living a life in which I can go for a jog or have a salad for supper – if that is what my body needs. However, it also means living a life in which I do not feel guilty if I sit around and eat spaghetti instead. Recovery allows me to relax without any feelings of rest-related restlessness wearing me down or tempting me to restrict. Recovery is a place somewhere between past trauma and future fear where I am free to simply enjoy being present, a place where I am not dominated by a disorder that developed out of a need to claim control. In that regard, maybe recovery is not a place after all, but a road, just as the age-old adage suggests. And in my case, I choose to refer to my road as a path.

This seemingly superficial change in wording is an essential (and intentional) aspect of my recovery. Furthermore, it is equally essential to point out that I see it as a path *of* recovery, not a road *to* recovery. Why does this matter? Because a path has a much different prescribed pace than does a road. We plod along pathways much more peacefully than we would speed down highways. Roads are destination-driven – we are going *to* a destination when we travel them. A pathway, on the other hand, is implicit of a process. Thus, whereas a traffic jam or detour might be seen as a setback on a speedway, an obstacle obstructing our path can be seen as an invitation for adventure. Furthermore, given my belief that recovery is a lifelong process, I would much rather spend the time I have left on this earth strolling peacefully down a pathway than I would dashing down an anxiety-inducing expressway.

There are two final attributes of these allegorical pathways that stand out as significant: their impermanence and unexpectedness. The best paths don't allow you to see very far ahead; instead, they curve through nature with surprises looming around every corner. That may be hard to accept for a control-demanding, destination-driven *disorderee*; however, with the right mindset, a little mindfulness and possibly a prescription or two, acceptance is achievable! When you finally accept that you are not going to be recovered tomorrow, and that you are only in control of the choices you make to confront the disorder today, you might just catch a glimpse of what recovery will look like for you.

Hidden within that final sentence is an allusion that might be enlightening if explored: Recovery happens in glimpses! In the early stages, these glimpses are fleeting and rare; however, as you continue along your path, I believe you will find that they not only start to linger a little longer, but also become guideposts that direct you when you hit one of those aforementioned forks. And since my mind works best in allegory, here is another of my metaphors to help explain this.

Most of us studied a language other than our native one. Personally, my means of linguistic torture was *Español*. While it didn't happen instantly, after fuddling with the foreign language and flunking countless pop quizzes, I unexpectedly caught a *glimpse* of comprehension one evening. I had been studying for a midterm all day, and upon drifting into dreamland, the dialogue that met me in my slumber was in – you guessed it – Spanish! I was dreaming in Spanish! It was surreal! Admittedly, I didn't wake up fluent, nor did I ace the exam, but I did catch a glimpse of what was possible if I kept studying. As such, Spanish was no longer foreign to me. The same is true with recovery. You are going to read books, hear different perspectives and test strategies that may seem foreign and possibly quite frightening – but if you persist through the pain, you will reach a point somewhere along the path where you catch a glimpse of what recovery looks like in your own life. These glimpses often come when you least expect them – such as when you spontaneously order a side of French fries while sitting at lunch with friends, or when you choose rest over routine by swapping out your gym bag for a TV remote. Maybe you'll be graced with a glimpse of recovery while reading this book – a feeling of freedom from your self-imposed isolation that comes when you reach a sentence that inspires you to leap up and yell, "YES! Me too!" These glimpses offer beautiful reminders that we are not alone – because you are *never* alone! So, whatever form it takes and whenever you catch a glimpse, go with it! Hold on to the hopefulness these instances incite and allow them to guide you as you approach the next fork that meets you on your metaphorical path.

These glimpses are exciting; however, their fleeting nature can be frustrating, and their impermanence can often leave us feeling like we are going in circles. I remember being taught as a child that the trick to not getting lost while hiking a new path was to simply keep turning right at every fork. This way, you will either end up circling back to your starting point, or a series of left turns can get you back home when you decide to turn around. These are great words of wisdom when backpacking in the woods, but the goal of recovery is *not* to backtrack. True, we may not know exactly where we are going, but backwards just isn't an option. So, when the pace of recovery seems painfully slow, or the cyclical nature of our struggles makes us feel like we are traveling in circles, remember that we are always moving forward. True, you may feel like you're backsliding when a bowl of cereal causes you to stumble in the same week that you overcome a bacon challenge at breakfast. You may feel like you are taking a step back when the anxiety of gaining a pound or two besieges you, despite your original goal of adding ten! You may be asking yourself, as we all do, *Why do I keep struggling with the same stupid feelings? Why do I keep stumbling over the same stupid steps? Why do I keep succumbing to the same stupid behaviors?*

Well, the answer to all those questions is the same: because recovery is *not* easy, and it is certainly not linear! That answer, easy as it may be, isn't nearly as fun as a little fable, though – so read on in the hope that it may help free you from any recovery ruts in which you may feel stuck today:

I'm walking down the road.
There is a hole in the sidewalk.
I fall in.
I am lost. I am hopeless. I get mad.
But it isn't my fault.
I climb out – bruised and beaten.

The next day I walk down the same street.
I approach the same hole in the same sidewalk.
I pretend not to see it. It is easier that way.
I fall in.
I can't believe I am in the same place.
I am furious, but it isn't my fault.
Someone put the hole here.
I whine. I scorn the situation.
But again – beaten and bruised – I find a way out.

The next day, I scurry down the same street...
Down the same broken sidewalk.
I see the hole, but I don't believe it is there. It is easier that way.
I fall in. It's a habit. I am good at habits.
I get mad. I get sad. I blame myself.
I know where I am.
I've been here before.
Beaten and bruised, I climb to the surface, and continue down the same
sidewalk.

The next day, I walk the same street.
I fall in the same hole.
But something changes this time.
I don't blame myself nor anyone else. I don't get mad.
I get motivated. I know the way out.
I am bruised, but not beaten.

The next day, I strut down the same street.
I see the hole in the sidewalk.
I acknowledge it.
I sidestep around it, and I keep walking. I have an idea...

The next morning, I set off down a different street.
I plot a new path. I made a choice – a choice to change.
I realize I can make choices. I smile.

My honest, heartfelt question for you is this: How long do you
want to wait before choosing another street? There is absolutely
no judgement written into those words – only empowerment and
encouragement. I want to encourage you because you have what it
takes to change course. More than encouragement though, I want
to empower you and support you by offering the assurance that I am
right here at your side – turning every corner and tripping over
every crack in the sidewalk with you.

As for walking in circles? There is no such option. It is impossible
to walk a circle in recovery, or in life. As the Greek philosopher

Heraclitus put it, "You cannot step in the same river twice." Our situations are always changing, and we are constantly growing. So, even when recovery seems repetitive, remember that what we often perceive as circles are actually spirals, corkscrews in which we get to choose whether we spin upward or downward. It's during this dynamic journey that we must decide whether we step in, around or over the *same* hole in the same sidewalk. True, we don't get to choose whether the sidewalk is broken, but we can mend our own brokenness by choosing to take a different route. We can rewrite our disordered destinies by plotting a different path!

Before continuing to the next chapter, take a moment to pause and reflect. Look around you. Take in your surroundings. Close your eyes. Inhale and envision yourself spiraling upward on the pathway of recovery – moving forward while forgoing the need to know exactly what *recovery* means or when the next fork might meet you. *Are you facing a crossroads today?* If so, where is it that you are hoping to go, and what choice can you make, in this moment, to guide you in that direction? Now exhale, breathing away any anxieties that come with making a change. This is exciting. You are recovering.

CHAPTER 22

THE CHESHIRE CAT CONUNDRUM

"Any road will get you there," that crazy cat claimed... but I call bullshit! Any road WILL NOT get you there – and now that we have a better understanding of where the "there" that we are traveling toward is, let us spend a few pages exploring the pathway leading up to the pathway of recovery.

We have already established that our friend Ed isn't actually a friend, and while it is important try to stay a little lighthearted in recovery, it is equally important that we recognize the severity of the disease. Pay attention to that change in language. We are not disordered, nor are we at fault for our afflictions; rather, we have been infected by a disease. It's a treatable disease, but a deadly one just the same. There are an infinite number of questions one could ask about the roots of this disease: *Is it genetic? Is it caused by trauma? Is it learned? Is it preventable?* However, at the end of the day, no answer would change the fact that we are infected. We have an illness – simple as that. And the longer we lollygag over questions about Ed's origins, the stronger the disease grasps us in the present. So, how about we allow the scientists and psychiatrists of the world to research the genesis of the disease while we focus our attention on overcoming it?

Recovery is a difficult and, quite likely, lifelong process. That's why I chose to call it a pathway. But, for as rocky as this path of recovery may be at times, it is often the path leading up to the path of recovery that is the most arduous... and alarmingly deadly! This *path to the path* is representative of what therapists refer to as the pre-contemplation phase of recovery. It's that painful purgatorial period during which the disorder has noticeably disrupted one's life, but recovery is not quite a reality yet.

By the time that I finally got help, a little over a month following that fateful physical I recounted earlier, I was so exhausted that I was nearly narcoleptic. I would spend hours dialing every residential center that I could find in a frantic attempt to escape the intense exercise regimen and restrictive eating practices I had imposed on myself after Ed kidnapped me. I was reaching out for help in all directions, but my path seemed to be nothing more than a series of dead ends.

"Hello, my name is Ryan, and I am struggling with an eating disorder. I was wondering if there was any way I could enroll in your program?" I'd pause for a second before adding, "Like, today?" I knew full well how absurd my requests were, but I was desperate and would do anything if it meant not having to wake up alone alongside Ed the following morning.

"I'm sorry, but we are completely full. I can get you started on the paperwork, though. Once that's completed and you get a medical evaluation, I can put you on the wait list." My heart would break. "We may be able to get you in as soon as next month."

Unfortunately, once you reach the point of admitting that you need help, there is not always such a thing as "next month." Everything must happen immediately. I was living in a state of constant panic – so intense that, at one point, I seriously considered committing a crime because being locked up would at least keep me safe from myself for a while. *Nothing too horribly heinous that it would wreck my career or life in the long term,* I thought, *but significant enough that it would land me behind bars for a few weeks.*

My lack of logic might be slightly laughable in retrospect; however, at the time, those thoughts were serious – and seriously scary! If it wasn't for the support of my family, friends and furry little four-legged sidekick, I doubt I'd ever have been able to navigate the dreaded path to the path of recovery. I would have become just another morbid statistic. What is truly scary is that, even with the support of those around me, the only thing that saved me in the end was a last-ditch trip to the ER.

I want to reiterate that those weeks leading up to the ICU were far from normal in the grand scheme of my existence. This is typical of the pre-contemplation phase of recovery. We can exist for years in a seemingly functional relationship with Ed until, all of a sudden, something happens to send us into a somersault. Ironically, that something is often the paralyzing decision to seek treatment.

Are you in pre-contemplation? Has your disordered eating finally destroyed enough of your life – or kept you isolated, anxious and exhausted long enough – that you are finally ready to confront it? Are your compulsive behaviors keeping you from living life in a way that prevents you from laughing out loud or lounging around on a Sunday afternoon? Has exercise become the excruciating focus of your day? Are late-night binges besieging your grocery bills, digestive system and ability to sleep? Are you finally fed up with Ed and ready to flip your middle finger at this infectious disease? Or do you love someone enough that you are ready to walk the path of recovery with them after they answer these questions?

If so, get ready, because I promise you that the path to the path of recovery is going to do its damnedest to beat the bejeezus out of you! The best defense you have is to anticipate it and lean on the shoulders of those who love you. Tell your friends and family that you are struggling and in need of their support. Then – and this is essential – allow yourself to receive it! These people will likely be foundational figures of your journey leading up to, enrolling in and leaving treatment... if you let them. Welcome others into the process because the more time you allow them to travel alongside you before treatment, the stronger your footing will be when you step out of it.

Are you scared to admit to others or yourself that you have an issue? If so, that's natural! However, I wouldn't worry too much because, as skilled as you may think you are at masking your disorder, Ed has likely shown his face to those who love you a long time ago. After all, the one redeeming factor about an eating disorder is that it is often one of the most visible of mental illnesses.

So, how do you prepare for the path to the path? Well, you can save yourself a little angst from the get-go by enlisting the aid of your insurance company. This will keep you from doing what I did:

cold-calling treatment centers and residential facilities that I could not afford or that could not accept me. The last thing you want when first reaching out for help is rejection, so turn some of the early investigative work over to the paid (and paying) professionals and focus your energy on you. Furthermore, recognize that nothing is likely to happen immediately on the medical side of things. It can take a little time to get things going; however, recovery needs to start today – not a month or two down the road. Thus, if you are ready to seek help, don't start by submitting yourself to self-destruction like yours truly. Instead, surrender to self-love. It is an all-too-common belief in the eating disorder community that, to receive care, one must make themselves the sickest they can possibly be. Don't do it! Treatment is not going to fix you – it is simply a tool to help you fix yourself. As you stare down your breakfast tomorrow morning, remember that the more broken you allow yourself to become in route to treatment, the harder it will be to put the pieces back together once you are in care. Finally, if you feel called to intervene in another's struggle, be prepared to support them through the initial shock and catch them if and when they stumble. Research possible recovery options before confronting a loved one so that your intervention can be seen as opening new doors, not closing existing ones.

The essence of an eating disorder lies in its deceitfulness. More simply put, an eating disorder lies! That is scary – and yet another reason why it is crucial to surround yourself with truthful people when you set off on the journey. As such, it is equally essential to accept that honesty often has a way of coming across as offensive or obtrusive. Don't push away when someone you trust says something that you don't want to hear. For this reason, my favorite leg of my personal stool of support will always be a paid therapist. Friends are fantastic, and family relationships can be fruitful, but none of us want to burden our loved ones with depressive and disordered thoughts. This is why friends and family will always fail in comparison to a good counselor, a safe someone with whom you can share all of your misery, routinely and in guilt-free fashion! Oh, and remember: A good therapist is *not* your best buddy, nor are they cheap… but they are worth the cost. YOU are worth the cost!

How many times have you sugarcoated the truth to appease a friend? (I apologize if that sweet-sounding choice of verbs was a trigger, although if it was, may be a good signal that it is time to seek some support!) How many times have you caved in to the request of a friend or family member to avoid confrontation? This is how the eating disorder works. It strengthens with every supportive relationship it severs, and it gains more control every time you allow its voice to speak louder than an honest ally. It is important to recognize that Ed is not your friend, and that a trusted therapist provides much firmer footing than your actual friends can, even when they have the best intentions. Ed's suggestions will always seem easier to digest than the meals you mull over, the counsel of a good therapist, or the concerned voice of a friend, but know that choosing him over all the others will only cause isolation and indigestion in the long run! All said and done, remember that – whether you are deep in recovery, contemplating it from afar or embarking on the super-scary path to the path – you are not alone. That is, unless you chose to face Ed alone; however, know that nothing good comes from being isolated with Ed!

Take a moment to map out your personal support system, like, right now! Go find a pad of paper and draw one of those organizational webs that you were taught to make in elementary school English class. Make yourself the subject by scribbling your name, big and bold, in a circle at center of the page. Then, draw several lines stretching outward from the central bubble, and on each one, write the name of a trusted friend, family member, counselor or the like. Which friends do you rely on, and which family members can you fall back on? Which friends or family members are not likely to risk straining your relationship by being truthful? What professional support do you have in place or need to seek out? Finally, and most importantly, are you ready to make that investment in yourself? Again, professional partners are not cheap, nor is their advice easy to hear, but you are worth it!

After you've mapped out your posse of supporters, take some time to list a few attributes of each potential ally. This will help you discern the areas of strength and weakness in your existing network. Who do you have that is good at planning? Who is good at listening? Who is good at enforcing? Whose shoulder is the most welcoming for a good cry? Once you have your support system mapped out, and you have accepted that your disorder is going to do its damnedest to isolate you from everyone on it, add me to your web! Allow your participation in my story to help you scribe and/or edit your own! Let our parallel paths serve as a reminder that your struggles are not your own – that you are loved, and that the world wants to see you well. Remember, too, that each page you read, write and live has the potential to push you one bite closer to health and wholeness.

CHAPTER 23

PLOTTING MY OWN PATH

"Two roads diverged in a wood, and I –
I took the one less traveled by,
And that has made all the difference."

– Robert Frost

"Hi. My name is Ryan, and I am an anorexic."

A euphoric rush flooded my soul upon first hearing my own voice openly admitting my ailment.

"Hi Ryan," the group of supportive self-proclaimed alcoholics replied in perfect unison.

Earlier that day, one of my housemates had encouraged me to attend his lunchtime Alcoholics Anonymous (AA) meeting, and, though I went into it planning to stay silent, it felt only fitting to admit my addiction when introductions rolled around. I hadn't known quite what to expect in doing so, but I was instantly overwhelmed by the nonjudgmental acceptance that this community had to offer. In retrospect, maybe I shouldn't have been so surprised – for one thing, anorexia does, after all, begin with an "a." However, in the 20 years I'd struggled with Ed, I had never found an eating disorder group that seemed nearly as supportive as that group did.

Allow me to backtrack a bit. Throughout this journey of mine, my somewhat unique living situation has proven to be one of the more advantageous aspects of my personal recovery. You see, in the two years leading up to my disordered downfall, I served as a live-in counselor at a 14-person sobriety home in Santa Cruz. Up until my return from residential care this past autumn, I functioned as a leader – a source of support for this tough group of addicts. Things changed upon my return home, though, and I found myself on the other side of the fence, forced to humbly receive their council. After all, if my residents had taught me anything over the years, it was that recovery only worked when it was rooted in humility. Thus, fresh out of residential care, I began to see myself less as a leader of the community and more as a member of the community – a partner on a parallel path toward wellness. And it felt amazing to have a few allies.

Prior to that initial AA meeting, I had always been a little skeptical of the way our world addressed drug and alcohol recovery. So, while I would encourage our residents to attend regular recovery meetings, the way the meetings started always seemed disempowering. *Why would anyone want to introduce themself by way of a past affliction, instead of their future aspirations?*

The answer lies in the importance of admittance and acceptance – admittance that our addictions are often stronger than our abilities to overcome them alone, and the non-judgmental acceptance of a like-minded group of friends who want to walk as one to ensure that no individual has to confront their issues alone. I've yet to experience this same sense of community in the world of eating disorder recovery. Our disorder remains too secretive, and our struggles are not as widely understood as those associated with drug or alcohol dependency. So, although things are improving, there has always been a certain stigma attached to eating disorders – not to mention, a shortage of support groups established to address them. And on the occasion that I do find a group, a strange underlying element of competition often overshadows any attempt at genuine camaraderie. So, whereas I had a multi-page printout of daily meetings posted on our house's refrigerator for my residents, when seeking support for my own addiction, I couldn't find but one weekly gathering. It was disheartening. Plus, that meeting had gone virtual with the COVID-19 pandemic, a time that proved a menace to mental health for more than just the recovery community.

In the weeks after my return from residential care, I began to bring the guys at the house into my personal recovery, just as they had sought my support through theirs. Up until that point, I had lived my life on the fringes, just some skinny, goofy guy bouncing between binging, restricting and over-exercising. And, let me tell you, neither the starvation nor exercise proved nearly as depleting as the effort to hide from a world that didn't understand my disorder! Take holiday dinners, for example. Everyone understands when alcoholic Uncle Ted abstains from the wine that is being passed around the table; however, no one gets it when their compulsive cousin Ryan pushes his peas around his plate for 45 minutes during that same meal. But that all started to change once I opened up to the broader recovery community. What I came to find was that I was not nearly as alone as I had once thought. I had found my tribe, my team, and I quickly came to appreciate the deeper relationship that I was forming with each of my housemates. True, our paths may not have been perfectly parallel – anorexia and alcoholism do have their share of distinctions – but they were not perpendicular, either. The opioid addict upstairs understood my exercise addiction, the alcoholic said "amen" when I opened up about my nightly binge, and the meth user had empathy for my midday restrictiveness. True, we were all very different, but we shared a commonality in that something beyond our beings had taken control of us. Now, the question was how to take back the reins.

If you find yourself craving community or experiencing eating disorder isolation, I encourage you to conduct a little experiment of your own. Do a quick search to find out what recovery meetings are being offered in your area. Then, step out of your comfort zone and into a community. You may never choose to make meetings a regular part of your recovery routine, or maybe you dive into one every day. Sometimes, just seeing the results from of a quick Google search is enough to offer a subtle reminder that you are not alone. Try it! After all, part of the premise of my pathway-to-recovery metaphor is that sometimes you must pave your own. Sometimes we must get creative in our processes. That might mean being the lone anorexic or food addict at a local AA or Narcotics Anonymous (NA) meeting. It might mean moving into a sobriety home as a transitional step out of residential care. It might mean any number of things, but what all those things have in common is that they are each an example of how we can reclaim control of our own destiny. I have no doubt that you will find increasing support and acceptance as you become a more active a participant in the broader recovery community. So, dive in with an open mind, a humble heart and an adventurous spirit – and never be scared to take "the [road] less traveled."

CHAPTER 24

FREEDOM

"Doing what you like is freedom;
Liking what you do is happiness."

— Sudha Murty

The sun was bright, and the seagulls swarming overhead seemed much hungrier than I was when I sat down for lunch on the Half Moon Bay harbor with a friend after my early exit from residential care. I was free for the first time in weeks. However, as I came to realize, it is difficult to enjoy good company, sunshine or a salty sea breeze when you're scared shitless!

In retrospect, I should have turned around and begged to get back into the program the second that I put my order of fried plantains in a doggy bag, but neither my ego nor my insurance company would allow that. As for the plantains? They were too sweet and greasy (or should I say, too good, gooey and tasty) for me to allow myself to enjoy them. DANGER!

"Aren't you going to finish your lunch?" My friend did her best to remain gentle in her inquiry, but the concern was evident in her voice.

"I'll save the rest for an afternoon snack," I replied in the sincerest of voices. DANGER! Lie numero uno: My daily snack was one of the first things I sacrificed upon escaping the watchful eyes of my dietitian, and I knew damn well that those plantains were destined for the dumpster. "We had a pretty big breakfast and midmorning snack before you arrived," I continued, defending my doggy-bag decision.

DANGER! Lie two: I had *conveniently* timed my visit to the nurse's office that morning to overlap snack, and breakfast was of average size.

"If you say so," she said with uncertainty. "I guess we can start heading back to Santa Cruz then."

"But it's so nice out and I've been cooped up for over two weeks. What do you say we go for a little walk on the cliffs first?" DANGER! The deceitfulness continued. Whereas a cliff walk would have been a pleasantly healthy option for a *normal* person, I knew full well that my underlying intention was to burn off a bit of the lunch I didn't finish. Thus, we will count this as lie three… and in any other context, that would constitute a strikeout!

I wanted to share this little exchange not to make myself sound deceptive, but to emphasize just how quickly Ed can take control of a situation. My intentions at the time had seemed harmless enough; however, it takes much more than a week or two of treatment to develop an awareness of whether it is Ed or our authentic self who is doing the talking. And on that day, it was all Ed. I had allowed the disorder to take the upper hand early on, and it would only be a matter of time before Ed reclaimed full control.

As it turned out, we did end up going for a very pleasant walk that afternoon, which I followed with a decent dinner. And, although I never did finish those plantains, I awoke the following morning with good intentions and a good appetite. Unfortunately, as the adage asserts, "The highway to Hell is paved with good intentions."

Hell may be an extreme description of the months to follow; however, re-entering the real world without a therapist, nutritionist or an outpatient program in place was about as unpleasant as a place could be – void of some flames and a red spandex-clad guy holding a pitchfork. I came to realize that leaving Half Moon Bay against medical authority was not only a poor recovery decision, but it also disqualified me from receiving any insurance assistance for future outpatient care. Thus, to use another common phrase, I was "up shit's creek without a paddle" – or a plan.

Actually, I take that back; I did have a paddle… and a kayak too! So, after lunch, I set out on Monterey Bay with the intention of paddling up some plans. Here is what I came up with:

1. **Walk only as far as my short-legged dog would.** Exercise has always been my Achilles heel, and walking aimlessly throughout the day was the easiest, calorie-consuming means of addressing my anxiety. Thus, by surrendering control to my lazy K-9 companion, I would be forced to find other, more constructive coping mechanisms. Furthermore, walking the dog qualifies as a mindful activity – the opposite of the mindless elliptical-machine miles I'd otherwise be logging. Finally, companionship was just what the hospital's psychiatrist had prescribed to counter my compulsive thinking.

   - **How did it work out?** Well, I did only walk so much as my dog would agree, and his persistent pee breaks proved to be a powerful lesson in patience; however, my bicycle commutes, kayaking excursions, surfing sessions and anxious pacing quickly pushed my activity level past the healthy range. Thus, in reflection, putting my pooch in control only counts as a half-success. That said, as an innocent side note, I do encourage everyone to adopt a dog in recovery because caring for another living creature provides a constant reminder that we too require love and care.

2. **"It's just lunch."** Upon entering residential care, I decided to welcome the world into my otherwise secretive struggles with a social media post about my inpatient admittance. Well, that post went viral, and the amount of support that I received left me awestruck. However, the funny thing about support is that it only works when you allow others to support you. Thus, my second idea involved a second post, this one requesting a few weeks' worth of lunch dates from my network of friendly Facebook followers. I had lived in Santa Cruz for more than five years at that point but had yet to venture out for lunch once during that span. So, knowing that midday meals could be menacing, I challenged my friends to take me for a tour of our city's best lunch spots.

   - **How did it work out?** It was kind of fun at first. The support was encouraging, and my calendar filled up quite quickly. However, it didn't take long before these daily dates wore me out. Being faced with constantly changing menus was a bit much, and the unavoidable anorexic elephant at the table put an awkward spin on the conversations that made the lighthearted lunchtimes I'd envisioned into something a lot heavier. In retrospect, I have come to find that it is better to focus less on food in early recovery. That doesn't mean eating in isolation, but making a big to-do out of lunch every day caused me to obsess about my midday meals. I now try to keep my breakfast and lunch as mindless as possible by keeping pre-portioned options easily accessible. That way, I can eliminate the indigestion that comes with the indecisiveness I feel every time I open my refrigerator. This saves mindful eating for supper, a meal during which I attempt to slow down and savor each flavor, because, in the past, a day of restriction would result in a nighttime binge. During both preparation and consumption, I make a conscious effort to pause periodically to explore my emotions, taste what it is I am eating and redirect my intention toward gratitude instead of guilt.

3. **Insert at least one wildcard food into my daily menu.** Being barraged by choices during that first meal of residential treatment revealed just how little diversity there was in my diet. For years, I had mindlessly meandered through the same aisles of the grocery store, picking up the same produce and pre-approved fare. As a result, my anxiety would spike whenever one of my familiar food options wasn't available. In response, I committed to add at least one unexpected item every day and venture into the unknown aisles of the supermarket on occasion.

   - **How did it work out?** Awesomeness! It turns out that I enjoy a lot of different foods! I quickly found friendship in sweet potato fries and companionship in cream cheese. The ironic consequence of this, though, was how quickly these once-wildcard treats became part of the compulsive menu that I was trying to disrupt! OCD is a close ally of disordered eating, so whether it shows its face in food, exercise or any other quirk of your day, I can't emphasize enough how important it is to switch up your routine.

4. **Stay conscious of my cabinets.** Another valuable insight gained in the kitchen of that Half Moon Bay home was how the amount of food around me influences my mood. I came to find that my anxiety spikes when I have either too much or too little food filling

the fridge, cabinets or table. It's a strange thing, really. I feel an anxious urge to eat everything in sight because I can't stand seeing food go to waste; however, I experience an equally intense urge to restrict from food throughout the day in an attempt to *earn* my ritualistic dinner, which comes with its own slate of anxieties. *Will I have all my ED food options available? Will I be able to eat alone? Will my schedule work out so I get home and feel hungry at 8pm? Will I have moved and/or restricted enough throughout the day to mute my guilt?* To address these anxieties, I have found it helpful to make several small trips to the grocery store each week and keep only a few days' worth of food in the fridge at any time.

- **How did it work out?** I got a smaller fridge!

Alright, so I had a few plans in place after returning from that paddle and, though none of them offered up the support, structure or reassurance of more traditional post-residential programming, it did feel good to have some parameters in place. Things went well at first. My housemates at the sobriety home got me plugged into the 12-step program, my dog regulated my walking, and even though my lunch-date idea turned out to be a little stress-inducing (not to mention expensive), it was helpful to have some sidekicks to lean on for support. The slipping started when the newness and excitement that I had initially associated with recovery began to wither into routine… and the aforementioned rut!

Approaching that first month of freedom as if I were embarking on some great adventure had kept my anxiety in check and encouraged me to continue confronting my compulsive behaviors. Every day I awoke in anticipation of a new challenge. As a result, my energy level remained high enough to allow me to approach each challenge as an opportunity to flex my recovery muscles. Unfortunately, as the days passed by, my escalating anxiety cast a cloud over the excitement that I'd initially attached to my journey. I started to lose my sense of adventure and my tolerance for discomfort. In turn, it wasn't long before my energy became devoted to preventing my next panic attack, rather than making any forward progress in recovery. Anxiety had again become my adversary, and I felt more alone every day that it continued to intensify. And it continued to intensify every day!

The sun was bright, and the air was fresh on yet another fateful morning on my path of recovery. Unfortunately, I was unable to enjoy either, having awoken with an all-too-familiar unsettled feeling in both my stomach and psyche – two facets of my being that have always been intrinsically, or obnoxiously, connected. My jaw tightened. I had started a dangerous dance of indecisiveness, and I knew that I had to choose how to approach the day before my wavering and worrying had the chance to take over. As such, I took guidance from a familiar little voice that encouraged me to flee from my feelings by biking to the cliffs on the northern end of town for an innocent little hike.

"It is a gorgeous day out, Ryan. You NEED to get out and take advantage of it."

It seemed like an innocent, even logical, idea at the time. Actually, on disorder days such as this, the simple act of making a decision is usually the best decision! Unfortunately, that familiar little voice that had tempted me with a hike was, of course, an old acquaintance named Ed.

Right around the time that I reached the trailhead, I felt the weather start to shift, and about a mile into my eight-mile adventure, the winds started whirling. The sensory stimulation was suddenly too much, and I panicked in response! The intensity of the wind on my face threw me into what I've come to refer to as a "trauma tunnel," and its dissociative effect was overwhelming. I attempted to push through it – to pause, belly breathe and address my anxiety through one after another of the long list of coping mechanisms that I'd picked up from various therapists over the years. Unfortunately, none of them could counter my kookiness that day, and, as my tunnel vision continued to tighten, that little adversarial voice that had advised me to go hiking that morning called out once more: "Run, Ryan... RUN!"

And I complied. Then, when I was done running, I skipped lunch. And after skipping lunch, I cried. Finally, after crying, I came to the gut-wrenching realization that I was not strong enough to do recovery on my own. As such, my fairytale recovery journey had ended. I was in trouble, and within a week, I lost all the weight that I'd put on during residential care.

So, you're wondering, *what did you do?*

I am glad you asked! I did exactly what any self-respecting 37-year-old guy would do: I called my mommy! (Remember how important humility is in recovery?)

Bless her heart, I hadn't so much as hung up the phone before my amazing 72-year-old mother loaded up the RV she'd purchased in celebration of her retirement and set across the country, from Maryland to California, to save her slightly insane, shrinking son from his downward spiral.

Was it a perfect solution? Not a chance! There are many issues that arise when utilizing your family and/or friends as recovery counselors. However, none of these issues could supersede the danger of dealing with my disorder in isolation.

Was it necessary? Most definitely! The only thing that I feared more than giving up control to my mother was knowing that I was in control of my own choices, because the reality was that I had lost control.

Did it work? Well… I am still typing, so I guess it didn't completely flop.

Did it affect the relationship I shared with my mom? Of course! But in a surprisingly beautiful way.

So, how did we do it? Well… knowing the importance of the ocean to my emotional well-being, my mom rented an Airbnb adjacent to the Santa Cruz harbor, which would become the site of our month-long, pseudo-residential reprieve. We then worked together to establish a three-meal-a-day diet, which we integrated into a schedule that balanced work, play and rest. We filled that playtime with constructive activities such as arts and crafts, visits with friends, and short recess breaks during which I could play in my kayak or walk the beach. Finally, we finished each day with an embarrassing personal favorite: a round of Candyland, a ridiculously cheesy board game from my youth that we had found buried at the bottom of our Airbnb's bookshelf!

Given the house's proximity to the frigid Monterey Bay, the best feature, by far, was the steamy hot tub that awaited my shivering body after periodical mental health plunges into the Pacific. It was summertime in Santa Cruz at the time, but in a city where summer is best described by the phrase "June gloom," we remained safely hidden under a chilly low-level cloud all month long. Every morning I would painstakingly prepare breakfast behind a curtain of fog. Then, after eating, I'd attempt to work for a bit to maintain some semblance of purpose and structure. However, given that my mind was about as foggy as the sky outside, I'd typically call it quits pretty quickly. Upon closing my computer, I would venture out into the grey abyss in my kayak, notably not for the multi-hour paddling marathons of my past, but for meditative floats alongside my canine first mate. When we'd return to shore, the two of us would dive into the icy ocean, then scurry back to the hot tub where we would await lunch. I've mentioned these playful plunges of mine several times now, and though they may seem like an insignificant inclusion, they have been one of the most essential components of my recovery and sanity. Over the years, I have tried a hodgepodge of medications, and just about every coping mechanism that I could Google; however, despite having studied psychology myself during my graduate work, the only thing that I've ever found that could truly reset my spirit is the shock of cold water. Skeptical? Test it out for yourself! Next time you get sideswiped by an anxiety attack or stuck in a depressive funk, simply find yourself a frigid body of water and bellyflop your way to bliss!

What's that? You don't live next to an icy ocean?

No problem! Just strip down, step into the shower, turn the faucet to freezing and wash your stress away! But I digress...

As those introspective days alongside my mother passed by, something interesting started to happen: I began to understand myself a little bit better. I started to see that my struggles were not so much centered around the act of eating as it was accepting that I was worthy of food, as well as the love of my own mother. I was too anxious to be productive, too emotionally fragile to have fun, and too scared of stumbling to take any solid steps on my own that month.

Thus, in retrospect, the most difficult aspect of those days was looking in the mirror and accepting that the fragile being who stared back at me was not only capable of healing, but worthy of it. This also meant accepting that pain is not an essential precursor to pleasure, that my self-worth is not measured by work or worldly success, that calorie consumption is not dependent on energy expenditure. And I had to accept that I was not broken – but that I *am* beautiful.

Harvard professor and world-renowned theologian Paul Tillich summed up these feelings better than any other in his book, *Courage to Be*. "The courage to be," he concluded, "is the courage to accept oneself in spite of feeling unacceptable." As I retrace my recovery journey thus far, the hardest part has not been eating, though forced feedings are far from fun. Instead, the difficulty comes with deservingness – being courageous enough to claim that I am worthy of food; courageous enough to accept myself, despite not fully understanding myself; and courageous enough to love myself, despite not always liking everything about myself. It takes courage not to blame oneself for a disorder, nor pity oneself for being afflicted with it, but to praise oneself for pushing against it. And the fact that you're reading this right now is a demonstration of that courage.

CHAPTER 25

"AUTOKTONÍA"

"Did you really want to die?"
"No one commits suicide because they want to die."
"Then why do they do it?"
"Because they want to stop the pain."
‒ Tiffanie DeBartolo, *How to Kill a Rock Star*

I titled this chapter with the Greek translation of a word which transcends language, time and culture: *αὐτοκτονία (autoktonía)*. That's because, while researching the New Testament of the Bible in graduate school, one verse stood out to me as particularly timeless, honest and relevant. "To live is Christ; to die is gain," Paul writes in a letter to the Philippines ‒ and not just "die," but αὐτοκτονία, or "choose to die." I love the way this verse so clearly acknowledges the undeniable fact that living is hard. Living is suffering. Living is a whole hell of a lot of work, and there are many instances in which dying might seem like a much more inviting option, especially for those who believe in eternal life and higher power. **Please do not take that as an invitation to throw in the towel,** but instead, a gentle bit of encouragement that you are not alone when you feel like the world is kicking your ass!

I confess that I was a little uncertain as to whether I wanted to share this next story with you all; however, given the statistics, I feel that the sociologically stigmatized subject of *suicide* is serious enough to warrant a couple of paragraphs… so, be forewarned, you are about to join me for a hike up the old "Stairway to Heaven."

The fog that morning was so dense that I couldn't see past the bow of my boat; though, in retrospect, my anxiety was so intense that I would have remained blinded to the world even in the clearest of conditions. I had left all my courage, as well as my dog, cuddled up alongside my mom, who was cozily reading a book in bed. Watching her son suffer over the previous few weeks had exhausted her, and I was struggling with the knowledge that I was causing her such strife.

"God, I wish I could be peaceful and lazy, too," I mumbled upon shutting the door and stepping out into the cold. Unfortunately, I didn't know how to be lazy. I didn't know how to give myself permission to rest or allow myself to be peaceful, cozy and warm. Besides, I went for a paddle every morning, and the fear of confronting my compulsive practices overshadowed my desire to lounge around with my mom, dog and a good book. So, I forged through the fog on my kayak.

I hadn't paddled but a few strokes past the harbor mouth before a wave of fatigue and depression washed over me. These were far from abnormal morning emotions, and I had often pondered just how much easier things would be if I didn't awaken the next day to meet them. However, up until this particular paddle, those thoughts had remained just that: *thoughts*. The closest I'd ever come to acknowledging any of these secretive suicidal inclinations was in marking the "Have you ever thought you'd be better off dead?" box on one of those questionnaires you get before a counseling appointment. It'd been nothing more than a philosophical ponderance at the time, but that quick click of my mouse set Kaiser Permanente's suicide prevention team on high alert, and my phone was flooded with follow-up calls for the next 24 hours.

So, no, I had never seriously considered suicide. I had simply danced lightly around the idea of throwing in the towel a time or two – but who hasn't? This world can be pretty damn daunting, and I'd imagine that just about everyone wandering its surface has hit a stretch at one point or another in which they wonder whether waking up the next morning is really worth it. But this time? This time was different. I had finally hit my breaking point. I'd lost hope and I was ready to call it quits. Yes, this time was more than a ponderance… today, I had a plan. Nothing too sophisticated, but it was dramatic, nonetheless. I would paddle out a couple miles, jump into the water and start swimming toward the horizon until hypothermia took me home − and we aren't talking about my mom's Airbnb. Done. Simple as that. I'd be paddling my way through the ol' pearly gates by lunchtime, leaving my dear friend Ed to shiver and sink into the depths of the ocean.

Tears of fear and regret formed in my eyes as I forged my way into the foggy abyss. I was so scared − scared to live, but equally afraid of the alternative. It scared me that I had a plan. Actually, I was more than scared… I was petrified. And as I continued to paddle out, panicked thoughts pounded me from every direction. *What if I can't silence the voice that is calling me to the sea? What will happen to my mom? To my dog? Am I really about to end my own life? Am I brave enough to end my own life?* I paused. *Am I brave enough to keep on living?*

I was trapped, doubtful as to whether I had the will to return to shore, but equally uncertain of my ability to pull the plug. That was precisely the moment in which a sharpshooting seagull snapped me out of my introspective trance with a revelatory splattering of slimy shit.

"Really!?" I hollered toward a God in whom I was quickly losing faith. *Talk about adding insult to injury,* I thought, while wiping this intestinal spitefulness from my forehead. "I'm finished. I'm Done. That's all folks. The end. The fat lady has sung, and the fat seagull has shat. You win!"

But just then, from deep within that moment of pain and peril, something strange happened. I started laughing. I laughed harder and louder than I'd laughed in a very long time. I laughed at myself and my *shit*-uation. *I wouldn't take my own life!* I thought. *At least, not as I had planned.*

Why, you may ask? Because diving into cold water was my secret strategy for regaining my sanity! Thus, as soon as I jumped into the ocean to end my life, logic slapped me back to my senses with his salty fist and left me chilly, wet and wading in the world of the living.

It felt good to laugh that morning, despite the morbid subject matter, and that little gift of intestinal fortitude was just what I needed to stop looking at life so seriously! I ended up returning from my paddle later that morning in rather playful spirits, hobbling the five blocks that separated our house from the bay after utilizing my ritualistic cold plunge to rinse the seagull shit from my hair. I was a pretty pitiful case: scrawny, soggy and shivering. But I was smiling! Actually, let me paint the full picture for you...

Just a few days before, I had strained my Achilles tendon while doing sprints in the sand alongside my pup, something I knew I should not have been doing! After that, the neighbors would watch me shuffle up and down the sidewalk each morning with a dog leash tied to one crutch and a pet poopy bag fastened to the other. The whole dog-and-crutch thing would have been okay had I stuck to the sidewalks; however, I made it a routine to take my pup on a short nature trail in route to our boat back in the days when I had two functional feet – and we all know what happens when an obsessive-compulsive anorexic gets locked into a routine! The trail itself was not too challenging – for the able-bodied hiker, that is – but it was not nearly wide enough for a pair of crutches and five clumsy feet (four of which were furry). Thus, every morning, I'd trip over a tangled leash as we traipsed the trail, only to repeat the dance upon returning from our paddle, hobbling to the beach for our prescriptive plunge.

"Don't you dare let that wet dog drag seaweed into the house again!" I heard my mother yell as I shivered toward the steaming hot tub.

"Yes, Mommy." I had to admit, it was fun to be an irresponsible brat again at age 37.

"And you better have washed your feet this time! If you get sand in that hot tub again, I'm going to..."

"Whoops," I mumbled under my breath, sweeping the sinking sand into the palm of my cupped hand before my mom came out with lunch. It wasn't my fault. I had gotten so cold crutching my way back to the house in the fog that I had, once again, waded into the warm water without washing.

This feels good, I thought, as gratitude tugged the corners of my lips into a smile. And I didn't mean the warm water – though that did have a heavenly effect of its own. Instead, I was thinking about the feeling that came along with being a little kid again – the simple and safe joyousness of having someone take care of you. We all need to be nurtured sometimes, to be kids again – irresponsible, slightly obnoxious and humbly helpless. That statement might seem contradictory, considering the crux of our disorder lies in our inability to surrender control, but I think it provides proof that, deep in our hearts, we know that we are completely out of control.

Every day that month, I hobbled my way up from the beach, heaved myself into the hot tub and waited for my mommy to serve up a surprise lunch. I doubt I will ever be able to express my gratitude for the support that my mother showed throughout those weeks, but the beauty of a mother is that you don't have to. It simply comes with the title. For as the Persian poet Hafez once wrote, "Even after all this time, the sun never says to the earth, 'You owe me.' Look what happens with a love like that. It lights the whole sky." What if you loved yourself that much? What if you could eat without feeling like you had to earn it? What if you could rest without first having to work out? What if you could accept the love of another for the simple reason that you are lovable?

That month was not only instrumental in helping me regain my footing, but it also offered up a vacation of sorts – a vacation from myself and my disorder. It was a vacation that reminded me of one of my favorite all-time movies…

"I feel good, I feel great, I feel wonderful… I feel good, I feel great, I feel wonderful… I feel good, I feel great, I feel wonderful." Bill Murray mumbles these scripted words of self-empowerment while walking to his psychiatrist appointment in the cinematic classic, *What About Bob.*

Bob, a middle-aged man overcome by OCD, is left anxious and alone when his doctor, played by Richard Dreyfuss, decides to go on a vacation to the lake.

"Baby steps, Bob," Dreyfuss says as he walks Murray out of his office and into the real world to face his disorder alone for a week. "Just take baby steps."

"I'm baby stepping! I'm doing the work, Doc. I'm not a slacker!" Bob makes his way toward the door, but before he can turn the knob, the reality of the real world hits him, and he falls to his doctor's feet. "Give me! Give me! I need! I need! Give me! Give me!" he cries.

This is how far too many of us approach treatment: "Give me a solution! Fix me! Give me an answer! Help me... because I cannot help myself!"

Needless to say, Bob's begging wasn't enough to keep Dreyfuss from his family vacation, but before sending Bob on his way, he gives him a rather peculiar prescription, not for a medication, but a meditation.

"It says, 'Take a vacation from my problems.'"

"That's right, Bob." Dreyfuss smiles. "A vacation from your problems."

Oh, if it were only that simple! If only we could take a vacation from our disorders, a lakeside siesta from Ed's incessant bantering! Well, why *can't* we? In all honesty, that is precisely what my mother allowed me to do, and knowing that it was only a temporary break was what made it successful. I wasn't ready to make a lifelong commitment to recovery at that point, so it pushed me through to know that I could return to my disordered ways if I did not enjoy the experience of eating, healing and existing *normally*. Logic assured me that my weight wasn't going to spiral out of control in only a few weeks, and I didn't have to fear being alone with Ed because my mother was right there alongside me. Most importantly, I knew that the life I was "vacationing from" had proven to be both unpleasant and unsustainable. So, I took a break!

What would it look like if you set off on a sabbatical from your disorder tomorrow morning? It might involve physical travel, but for most of us, it would simply mean submitting to a cognitive staycation. What would you do with your day if you woke up uninhibited by the must-dos of your ED? Would you roll over in bed and catch up on a little shuteye if you didn't need to sneak in a sunrise workout? What would you fix for breakfast if you were allowed to eat – and enjoy eating – anything that you craved? What would you do with all that creative energy if it was not corrupted by your compulsive behaviors? Maybe you would paint a picture. Maybe you would read or write a book. Maybe you would lie on your back and make creatures out of the clouds. The possibilities are endless – or, as endless as you allow them to be.

It goes without saying that a vacation will never be a forever fix – after all, the essence of a vacation lies in its impermanence. Thus, at the end of that month alongside my mommy, the time came for me to go back to being a big boy in the real world. Unfortunately, at the time, the real world was really complicated because of the COVID-19 pandemic. All the usual resources were in quarantine. This meant there were no in-person therapy options, no in-person support groups, and no one would answer the phone at any of agencies I dialed seeking support. The world was in isolation mode – and isolation is an eating disorder's best bud.

CHAPTER 26

LIMPING ALONG ALL ALONE

Recovery, for me, might best be defined as one of those obnoxious revolving doors found in an airport or office building – and that disordered not-so-merry-go-round had only sped up once I decided to face my adversary. I was stuck in an obnoxiously exhausting spinning threshold, unable to escape through the same side I entered (relapse), but too timid to step out the opposing exit (recovery); unable to accept a life alongside Ed, but too intimidated to leap into a new reality without him. Thus, I found myself stuck in a sadistic spin cycle, taunted by the freedom of the future, but unable to escape the painfulness of my past.

I had started off on a good foot following my mom's visit, which is a good thing considering I only had one functional foot at the time. My weight was on the rise, my motivation was up, and a month of nourishment had helped to mend my mind. Unfortunately, as my health improved, so too did my energy level, and I started to struggle with finding peaceful, purposeful, non-exercise-oriented ways of expending it. I was still on crutches at the time, which would force any logical human being to rest; however, I've proven by this point that logic is not one of my virtues. Thus, I proceeded to push past my body's physical limitations once again.

The ocean was calling out, and in response, I started dabbling into the world of one-footed surfing. Nothing too intense – just a wave or two to boost my mood. And good God, did my return to the salty sport feel great!

I can do this recovery thing... I can eat three meals a day! I can gain a few more pounds. I can be a functional human being! My resolve had returned, and it appeared as though I had dodged another injury-induced relapse! Unfortunately, what I found was that all those confident "I can" clauses were dependent on external circumstances. In other words, every "I can" came with an "if." I *can* eat three meals a day... *if* I get in a good surf session. I *can* keep my motivation up... *if* life continues to flow in the right direction. I *can* be a functional human... *if* the weather, my schedule and my dog cooperate. *I can* make healthy decisions... *if* I feel healthy that day. Finally, I *can* surf on one foot... *if* the wave isn't too big. Unfortunately, one early autumn swell annihilated that particular "if," and we all know what comes next: WIPEOUT!

I remember watching the wave form over my left shoulder. It was a perfect head-high crest of ocean coming to take me for a ride. *Paddle, paddle, paddle!* I hopped up onto my one good foot as I felt the pulse of the wave propel my board forward. But the wall of water had grown a little larger than I'd expected, and I wasn't quite fast enough on one foot to escape its fury.

With the splash came a *crack*. I still don't know if the sound came from my surfboard or my rib because I broke them both. Either way, I knew that it wasn't a good noise. I had promised my mom when she left that I wouldn't pick up a surfboard before picking up three more pounds, so some might call it karma that caught me in water that day. Whatever it was, it hurt, and injuries had always been detrimental to my recovery. I was still unable to walk without crutches, but thanks to a freshly broken rib, I couldn't walk *with* them, either. And I quickly came to find that I had yet to figure out how to confront my anorexic anxieties without walking or surfing.

No big deal, I thought. *I'll simply cut back on the calories for a few weeks while I recover, and then I'll pick things up again once I re-up my activity level.* No harm done... right? But a little less lunch is not a very recovery-minded mentality; thus, once again, my crippled body soon fell into another downward slide. I had gotten myself stuck in that damn revolving doorway once again, and I was getting dizzier every time I circled between recovery and relapse.

True, my weight had inched up after a month of mom-made and monitored meals, but those few pounds I'd put on only granted me a false sense of security, not the reserve necessary to stay healthy or sane on a shrinking diet. Thus, my anxiety began to ramp up as the numbers on the scale slid down over the course of the week to follow. I had officially and unwillingly invited Ed back into my life – and that was an invitation that he wasted no time accepting.

I didn't spiral completely out of control this time around, and both my foot and rib did heal in the weeks to come. There were days during that month when I did pretty alright, though there were more days during which I did not. There were a few times when I laughed and felt alive, but there were many more when I cried and questioned whether I wanted to live. There were fleeting moments when I felt free, but they were interspersed with long hours of feeling imprisoned. There were instances of hope, but, overall, hopelessness had regained its hold on me, and it was slowly taking its toll.

"I've seen you out surfing and biking quite a bit lately, Ryan," my doctor said as I stepped off the scale during my monthly check-in. Santa Cruz is a pretty small town, so it was hard to hide my activities from a fellow outdoor enthusiast. "I thought we were taking some time off?"

"I'm eating more." I paused. It had been a blind weigh-in, so I didn't know the exact numbers, but the frown on her face was a telltale sign that my weight had dropped to a dangerous level. "Well... I am trying to eat more. It's just... my anxiety. It has been out of control again, and it is too intense to sit with." She'd seen me surfing and had watched my long walks on crutches, but she wasn't aware of the gym workouts that I had snuck back into my schedule every other evening.

"When are you going to start taking this seriously?" She paused to make sure she had my attention. "You know that the statistics are not in your favor, don't you? Do you really want to be just another number? Another victim of the disease?" Her words sat heavy in my empty stomach. "And as for your anxiety, that is your nervous system's way of telling you that your body is underfed and overworked. Any attempt to exercise or starve it into silence is only going to make it scream louder."

I believe wholeheartedly that the universe sends us messages to guide us along our way as we wander through this world. Whether or not we heed them is up to us. In the week to follow that discussion, the universe tried hard to tell me to slow down – to the point that it once again called on Poseidon to help! After my doctor echoed my mother in restricting my surfing, I snuck out for three more surfing sessions – and snapped two more surfboards, dinged my forehead and damaged my ego in the process. I also blew out two tires during evening bike rides and spent a good two hours each morning wrestling with starvation-induced writer's block while staring at the same stupid paragraph of the book you are reading today. I was slipping and forgetting all the painstaking lessons that I'd learned on my journey thus far. I'd stopped meditating, I'd stopped praying, I'd stopped painting, and I'd begun playing with fate. And fate is a fatal playmate.

CHAPTER 27

A RESIDENTIAL REPLAY WITH A PSYCHEDELIC TWIST

"Life is a series of natural and spontaneous changes. Don't resist them, that only creates suffering. Let reality be reality. Let things flow naturally, whatever way they like."

– Lao Tzu

"When are you finally going to free yourself from this self-defined *anorexic purgatory* you are trapped in and go back into residential treatment?"

What the hell!? I was stunned! I couldn't believe what I was hearing. *Was I really paying $190 per hour for a 50-minute therapy session, just to be told that our therapy sessions were not enough?*

"Or maybe you simply enjoy making things more difficult than they need to be?"

"Huh?" It took me a few seconds, but I managed to muster up a sad, single-syllable response to her query. It wasn't that I needed my therapist to repeat the question – I hoped she wouldn't! I simply didn't know what else to say.

"How much longer are you going to tiptoe around those ten painstaking pounds that YOU admitted you needed to gain before you finally wave the white flag and surrender to a little assistance?"

"January 1st." I was uncertain if her question was hypothetical or literal, but I answered it regardless. It was September 2, 2020, at the time, four months after my early escape from that first round of residential care, and four months ahead of the date that I'd consider returning to it. And, while it is true that I hadn't made any significant progress during those first four months of freedom, I certainly didn't plan on going back to captivity! It wasn't the weight that scared me. I wanted to be *at* my goal weight. It was the discomfort and unknowingness associated with the process of getting there that plagued my soul. Just the same, it wasn't the thought of being in residential treatment that kept me from seeking help. It was the pain-in-the-ass process of getting accepted, getting screened, getting my life in order enough to leave it behind, and getting my obnoxious insurance company to write a referral. Thus, for the time being, I would continue to "make it hard on myself" by pushing my anorexic boulder up recovery hill all by myself.

"January first," I repeated, with a little more confidence this time. "If I haven't gained ten pounds by the new year, then I'll consider re-entering residential." Not only did that give me four months to gain a few pounds, but it put the thought of a residential rerun far enough into the future that I didn't have to accept the reality of it in the present.

"Deal." My therapist stuck out her hand for a conformational shake.

***

That age-old adage I mentioned about pushing boulders up hills is actually quite relevant in recovery, and the stupidly stubborn side of us that it represents might best be examined via a brief comparison of Eastern and Western perspectives of *struggle*. In the Western world, we seem to seek out struggle and praise those who push the biggest boulders up the steepest hills.

"Push harder," we proclaim.

"The greater the obstacle, the more glory there is in pushing past it," declared Molière.

"It's part of life to have obstacles. It's about overcoming obstacles; that's the key to happiness," wrote Herbie Hancock.

That's all fine and dandy, I guess, but just where has that stubborn mindset landed Western society? Anxious, exhausted and addicted to pain meds and anti-depressants! Oh, woe be us, the workaholic Westerners, who take pride in pushing heavy things up steep hills.

In contrast to Western stubbornness, Taoist-rooted Eastern traditions see struggle as a sign that it may be time to take a new path. The teachings of the Tao (or "the way") counter the Western notion that success requires struggle. Instead, they encourage people to use their intuition and follow the natural order of the universe when discerning their direction – or, in our case, when re-ordering our disorders. The goal is to align with the natural flow of life in a way that allows the individual to operate on the principle of minimal effort – the natural world flows perfectly and effortlessly, after all. As such, hindrances to the natural order, aka disorders, are merely consequences of humankind's obsessive need to overthink EVERYTHING. In other words, we disrupt the natural order of the universe when we try too hard to control it and/or function off ego instead of intuition. And our egos enjoy pushing these enormous boulders just about as much as our cleverness delights in devising crafty ways of outsmarting our impediments and over-analyzing our disorders. Again, this is awesome in a society that praises pushing around heavy things; however, if you've reached a point of anorexic exhaustion, take a tip from the Tao and let the rock tumble for a change.

***

Fast-forward four months after I promised to stop pushing my unrelenting anorexic boulder up a hill, and I cringed as I looked down at the scale, then back at the calendar on the wall of my local gym. December 30th. Not only had I failed to gain those ten pounds, but I had lost three in the process. It was the first time in a long time that I had weighed myself without a doctor or therapist present to keep me from freaking out, and the numbers sent me into a downward spiral. The more I focused on my weight in the weeks to follow, the further it fell. The further it fell, the more hopeless I felt. The more hopeless I felt, the less able I was to confront my exercise compulsions and restrictive eating patterns (i.e., I moved more and ate less.) As a result, I'd lose another pound, and the cycle would start over once again: panic, hopelessness, food restriction, increased movement, another pound. If that wasn't enough, my therapist had disappeared earlier that month to care for her dying father and left me all alone during an already difficult holiday season. It was then that I realized how sick I had become because, instead of feeling sympathy for her struggles, I only felt angry that I had been left alone.

So, what did I do? I picked up the phone and made the call that I had committed to making four months prior.

"A month!?" My heart broke. "Yes, put me on the waiting list," I said to the admissions director of the same residential home in Half Moon Bay that I had passed through some eight months prior. I was scared – and the panic that I had felt leading up to my first inpatient experience returned in full force. I had officially relapsed.

"Great. You're on the list." She paused. "But we will need you to get medical clearance and a referral before we can actually accept you."

Fuck, I thought, as I recollected what it had taken to get referred to residential that first go-around. I was right back where I started; however, I had learned a lot from my first experience, and I knew that it would take all that wisdom to keep myself from self-sabotaging while I waited to be admitted.

I tried everything to ease my anxiety in a frantic attempt to escape my thoughts in the weeks to follow. I booked airline tickets to Hawaii, thinking that a physical change of scenery might magically pacify my panic; however, I cancelled them soon after because I was too anxious to travel. I researched yoga teacher training retreats, thinking that a month of pre-portioned vegan meals and guidance from stretching swamis might calm my compulsive behaviors; however, I couldn't commit to any of them. I applied for a Buddhist work-trade program in the hope that I might meditate and garden my way to wellness; however, when accepted, I made excuses for why I couldn't attend.

I even participated in a mushroom-enhanced intensive breathwork session upon reading about the use of psychedelics in eating disorder recovery – allow me to pause and reflect on that particular experience in a little more detail.

The session started with me pulling a tarot card, which was and is a foreign practice for most Christian ministers. But given my sense of spiritual curiosity, coupled with my disordered desperation, I was quite open to it.

"Ah yes, the base Chakra," my guide explained while I stared at the glowing pelvis of a cartoonish figure sitting in lotus pose in the middle of the colorful card. "That is your adrenal chakra."

I flashed back to the conversation on adrenal fatigue that I'd had with my integrative doctor just a few weeks prior. "Interesting," I responded as the guide went on to explain that pulling the base chakra card meant that my basic needs for survival weren't being met. Little did he know how fitting that card was in defining the starving soul that pulled it!

The guide repeated the ritual with the other nine individuals in the room before eventually passing around a ceremonial shell filled with psilocybin (mushroom) capsules. When the shell made its way to me, I took a breath, popped a few in my mouth and muttered off a quick prayer of forgiveness as I swallowed, hoping that I hadn't offended God by playing with psychedelics or tarot cards.

"Come play with me!" Before I knew it, I was lying on my back, practicing short, rhythmic belly breathing face-to-face with my six-year-old self. "Come play!" the child insisted as he extended an open hand. It was a version of me that I had long since forgotten. The me who existed before the death of my father and birth of my disorder – the authentic me. It was the me who existed before the world had told me who to be. It was a me whose voice had grown faint in the three disordered decades to follow.

"Play with me."

I stretched out my hand, but I couldn't reach his. I tried to speak, but no words would come out. Instead, I did what all grown men would do while spinning on psychedelics… I cried. "I can't," I finally yelled out, uncertain as to whether I was lying on the floor of the present or in the yard of my childhood past. His hand was so close, but as much as I yearned to embrace it, I just couldn't quite grasp it.

"You have to give up control, Ryan." The faint voice of my present guide came through clearly, despite the fact that I was engulfed in an intense encounter with my past. "Relinquish control and surrender to the flow." Those words continued to echo through my mind; however, as much as I wanted to, I still couldn't touch the fingers of my innocent former self. And, though I am sad to say that I was not able to relinquish control and go play with my inner child that afternoon, I did leave that session with a new sense of perception.

I share these slightly nontraditional ideas and experiences as examples of the diverse paths one can take toward recovery, as well as to demonstrate just how desperate I was during those weeks spent waiting until I could retreat to a residential environment that I both despised and desired. I waited to curl up and hide in a house that could keep me from hurting, starving or sitting alone with myself – I was waiting for recovery to come to me. But, as I have said many times before, recovery must start in the present, and with us walking toward it first.

It was Christmas week 2020 when the call finally came in from Half Moon Bay. It looked like the wait was over! I wasted no time in scheduling a physical for the following day and, after giving all sorts of excuses for my early discharge that previous summer, I managed to finagle a referral from my psychiatrist. *Maybe I am finally in the flow,* I thought, as the ease with which things were unfolding caught me off guard. At this rate, I would be in treatment before the new year! I finally felt at peace. Still, I awoke the following morning with a tightness in my chest. Not from anxiety, but...

Ring, ring, ring... "Hey Brent, how are you holding up?" I had just performed a burial-at-sea memorial service for a friend's father several days before, and I was curious to hear how he was doing.

"I've got the COVID virus, Ryan," he said in lieu of a salutation. "I'm sick as a dog, dude. You feeling okay?"

No! Not now, I thought, as my heart plummeted, and my chest further constricted. Contracting COVID would not only bar me from treatment for another month or more, but it would also force me into quarantine, a prescribed isolation during which I would be forced to sit alone with my thoughts, urges, anxieties and anorexic idiosyncrasies for 14 days. That would be two weeks in isolation with Ed!

"I, um… well actually, I'm…" I knew then that I had the stupid virus, and I was scared to death of what that meant. "Actually, I am not feeling so hot, either."

I had indeed contracted the cursed COVID-19 virus, and, while the flu was not all that severe in itself, the effects of quarantining alongside Ed were disastrous. I lost five pounds in those two weeks, a period which could best be described as a depressive 14-day panic attack. Furthermore, I was forced to surrender my spot on the waitlist at the Half Moon Bay house until I could test negative for the virus, a hurdle that could take several more weeks to clear. I had all but lost hope when, out of the blue, I received a phone call from a friend who knew I was struggling.

"Listen, Ryan, I recently got a little bit larger settlement than I had planned on, or needed, from that accident that I had last year." My friend Dave had been hit by a car while walking his dog the previous spring, and though he and his pooch were back in perfect health, his lawyer had made sure they profited from the punitive damages. "I would like to use it to cover some of your treatment costs."

"I don't know, Dave… I mean, that's really generous and all, but…" Under normal circumstances, my ego – coupled with my intrinsic sense of un-deservingness – would stand in the way of accepting his offer; however, I was desperate, and desperation is a strong antidote. "Well, let's chat about it tomorrow."

"It's worth the cost to see you smile again," he added before hanging up.

I had been researching alternative programs for days after having lost my waitlist position, so I started making calls as soon as our conversation ended. Admittedly, I was a bit pessimistic, but that quickly changed when a West Hollywood eating disorder and addiction recovery center offered me a scholarship that would allow me to spend 30 days in their care. The program had immediate space for an eating disorder client after having experienced several unexpected discharges the week before, and they agreed to subsidize my costs – if, and there was a big if, I could make it there before the weekend.

It was now or never. It was Thursday afternoon when I hung up the phone, and that meant that I had less than 24 hours to get my life together enough to leave it behind for 30 days. I started packing before even hanging up the phone. I was going to get help! And as I dropped my pup off at a friend's house for a prolonged playdate, I felt a strange feeling: hope. However, as we've come to learn by now, hope can be a dangerous thing.

CHAPTER 28

RECOVERY FANTASIES DEFUNCT

"It is not the strongest of the species that survives, nor the most intelligent, but the one that is most responsive to change."

– Charles Darwin

I arrived in West Hollywood the following evening after sneaking in one last sunrise surf session, skipping lunch and singing my way through the six-hour southbound drive. However, what I quickly came to find was that the program to which I had committed myself (and $15,000) was a little *less* restrictive than your average residential care facility. Thus, I could hear Ed cheer upon arrival when the intake coordinator asked me if I "would *like* to eat dinner." Then I felt him dance with joy when we caught sight of the unmonitored staircase just outside the back door of my dormitory. Intuition told me right then that I was in trouble; however, I am an expert at ignoring intuition, so I settled on a banana with a dab of peanut butter in lieu of dinner before making my way to bed.

I could attempt to summarize the saga that unfolded over the following weeks for you, but I feel that sharing some selected journal entries might provide a more personal perspective. So here ya have 'em: Ryan's disordered diary dialogues. Enjoy!

DAY 1

Dear Journal,

I had to surrender my computer upon arriving last evening, so it looks like it is just you, me, a pen and some paper for the next 30 days. I must admit, this is not the shiny, star-studded introduction to Hollywood that I initially hoped for – and even as I scribble these words, I admit that I am a little nervous for what this month may have in store.

It is only the first day, but this morning I woke up starving after making a not-so-recovery-minded decision to substitute some fruit and peanut butter for supper last night. I wasn't planning on skipping my first meal here, but they gave me a choice! And the reason for my return to residential treatment is that I cannot be trusted to make recovery-minded choices! If the leniency in meal enforcement wasn't enough to induce a little initial anxiety, the unmonitored staircase looming outside the door of my dorm sure as hell is! It took some work, but I dodged the desire to run stair-repeats this morning by doing some sun salutations to welcome the dawn. Yeah, I know... I shouldn't be running stairs or performing sun salutations on my first day of recovery. I should be recovering! However, I *needed* to do something to address the anxiety that came with knowing that I'd be eating and sitting the rest of the day.

By the time our breakfast cart arrived, I was famished! Famished, and confident that I could handle whatever it was that the team would serve up. Pancakes, pastries or protein shakes – bring it on! I was ready for anything! I was going show Ed who was the boss of breakfast! Unfortunately, what I wasn't ready for was another choice. And before I could decide what it was that I *should* eat, Ed had garnished a small bowl of bran flakes with a strawberry and set it on the table in front of me alongside a little kiddy-carton of skim milk. Ugh. I was starving, but too bewildered to battle over breakfast. I'd do better with snack.

Well, midmorning came quickly, and my indecisive anxiety once again overcame my appetite. A single stick of string cheese: that was all I could muster up the might to munch on. The scary thing was that the staff was okay with this! Thus, after starting off my day with an elongated yoga session, skimping on both my morning meals and declining dinner the night before, I feel as though I have likely lost a pound since my arrival – not to mention, any semblance of control, confidence and/or cognition. Ed is laughing pretty damn loudly at the moment, and I am nervous that it may be too easy for him to act out at this place.

What happened? A few months ago, I was able to finish every meal in its entirety when faced with the hospital's strict nutritionist. However, now that I have a little freedom of choice, I can't seem to help but to skimp, skip or scheme my way deeper into malnourishment. FRUSTRATION! A couple of months ago I had been able to make it through a series of sedentary days doing nothing more than a little mindful movement while up in Half Moon Bay, but now, less than 24 hours upon my arrival here, I'm being taunted by that demoralizing set of stairs every time I walk out the door. Ugh!

Meals and stairs aside, let me at least fill you in on the program that I'll be participating in for the next month. Our day starts with breakfast at 8am. Actually, as I already mentioned, my day starts much earlier with a few salutations to welcome the sunrise, but that is my own disordered decision. After breakfast, we pack into a van and drive downtown for seven hours of clinic. Clinic can best be described as an array of private, group and occupational therapy sessions, broken up by two snacks, lunch and a meditation. I am actually looking forward to the group sessions this month. They should offer an interesting dynamic given that they interweave individuals overcoming alcohol and drug addictions with eating disorder recovery folk like me. This cross-pollination of kookiness was one of the draws of the program, as I've found that I often relate better with the AA/NA guys living at the sobriety house that I manage than I do with other ED patients. Needless to say, the confusion caused by this grouping led to a rather comedic introduction this morning...

"You came here to work on your ED?" An inquisitive heroin addict questioned my enrollment in the program. "You seem young for that..."

"Young?"

"Yeah," he continued, after an awkward pause. "I mean, my grandpa jokes about his erectile dysfunction, but I don't know many people in their 30s who talk about theirs publicly – let alone see it as a reason to go to rehab."

"Ha!" I burst into laughter. "I don't have **e**rectile **d**isfunction." I playfully corrected my neighbor. "I have an **e**ating **d**isorder."

That humorous misunderstanding not only provided a welcome break in an otherwise anxious morning, but it also shed light on the ignorance of our society regarding eating disorders amongst the male gender. That said, maybe the joke was on me... after all, one of the long-term consequences of an eating disorder is a diminished sex drive!

For the time being, it looks like lunch is ready. So, let us forego any further discussion of my phallic functionality and allow that little bit of laughter to serve as a precursor for what looks to be a rather an interesting month instead!

Until next time,
Ryan

DAY 4

Dear Journal,

Well, I made it to day four, though I fear I may be, for lack of a better word, fucked. Today was the third day in a row that

I gave in to a sunrise stair workout and, once again, failed to compensate for it at breakfast. It started innocently enough. Just a quick ten-minute jaunt to get my heart rate up and ease some of the anxiety with which I'd awoken. But good God, did that ten minutes feel great! So great, in fact, that those ten minutes doubled the following morning, before becoming half an hour today. It's not as though I don't know better. In fact, "knowing better" often ruins my workouts because the guilt that comes with consciousness only amplifies the anxiety that I'm trying to exercise off.

Evenings here are particularly hard and lonely. Without a computer, I can't turn to work for distraction – and without a phone, I can't call a friend for companionship. I don't seem to fit in very well with the other clients in the program, so I spend most of my free time sitting alone with my thoughts in the shadow of that stupid staircase. I have tried to fill my idle time with more formative activities, but with little success. So far, I have bruised a bushel's worth of lemons trying to juggle, broken two strings while strumming my guitar and painted pretty pathetic pictures that have since become snack-time placemats. I am less than a week into a 30-day commitment, and already I am counting down the minutes until I can reclaim my freedom – though the reality of freedom is but a false facade. Panic!

On a more positive front, whether I like to admit it or not, I am learning a lot from my time here. Take, for instance, how boredom and the perception of confinement correspond to my compulsive exercise and eating habits. When I feel unproductive or indecisive, I turn to movement in the false belief that movement equals productivity. Furthermore, when I feel confined by a system, such as the 9am-to-4pm clinical component of this program, I try to reclaim control by restricting food. I brought this need for nonconformity up during a therapy session today, and here is how it played out...

"We have to figure out where your constant need to push against authority derives from," my therapist said, trying to dissect my disorder. "You are constantly coming up with ways to escape externally imposed rules by creating your own internal set of rules, which prohibit you from pushing back on what truly has you trapped: your eating disorder!"

I nodded in anxious anticipation of his miraculous solution for my oxymoronic situation.

"Every time that you push against an external restriction that's meant to help you recover with an internal one created by Ed to keep you sick, you give strength to the disorder." He paused to let this sink in. "In other words, every time that you declare, 'I won't be controlled' by a person or program which you perceive to be restrictive, what you are actually claiming is, 'I can't challenge my disorder.'"

I hated to admit it, but he was right. Three days ago, I ran those stairs for ten minutes as a means of proclaiming, "I won't be confined by a program." Then, today, upon climbing out of bed, sore and still half asleep, my eating disorder declared, "I can't take a day off my morning stair workout routine." Yesterday, I silently shouted, "I won't eat snack," after a group session went longer than expected and threw off my meal routine. Then, today, a voice from inside insisted that "I couldn't eat snack," much to the chagrin of my growling stomach.

So many of my disordered decisions can be traced back to the false belief that I can't challenge my compulsive behaviors. However, as my therapist pointed out, each submissive "I can't" originates as an anti-authoritarian "I won't." "I won't be confined by the rules and restrictions of society" because "I can't break my own rules or live unrestricted." The question now is: How do I push against my disorder with the same force that I am pushing against a program that was established to help me overcome it? How do I say to Ed, "I won't run stairs tomorrow morning," or "I can't skip snack tomorrow afternoon"? The anxiety induced by simply scribing those words is enough to let me know that I have a lot of work to do; however, for the time being, it is snack time. And I can't skip snack!

In hope and uncertainty,
Ryan

DAY 8

Dear Journal,

Today is the fourth day on a new anti-anxiety medication... and I feel pretty damn flighty. I am a little dizzy and a bit nauseous – two "common early side effects" of anti-anxiety medications that do an excellent job of exasperating an already anxious person's anxiety! Over the course of the last several months, I have been prescribed several medications, but I have not been able to stick with any of them long enough to allow them to balance in my system. Thus, even if I gain nothing else from this little Hollywood experience, at least it provides a safe and supportive setting in which I might be able to push through the unpleasantness that SSRIs (selective serotonin reuptake inhibitors) have been known to cause.

Ever since high school, I have had a love-hate relationship with anxiety medications – and, as a result, I have been on and off quite a few of them. I love the peacefulness that I feel when my panic finally subsides, but I hate the emotional apathy and brain fog that many of these medications cause. I love the elation and excitement of my non-medicated manic moments but hate the depressive dips that come when my mania wanes into anxiety. Thus, I have spent a large part of the last two decades bouncing between the exuberance of emotional irregularity and the sleepy state of SSRI stability.

That little ditty may have worked alright in the past (though that's open for debate), but it seems as though malnourishment has finally taken its toll this go-around and messed with my body's ability to properly metabolize medications. As a result, I have been unable to push past the first flighty weeks of my psychiatrist's prescriptive protocols on my own in the real world.

"What you're feeling is pretty normal," the program's psychiatrist said to reassure me that I wasn't going crazy (or that my craziness wasn't worsening). "SSRIs are metabolized in the stomach – and since eating disorders mess with one's metabolic system, the medications often don't work as they should until one's weight is restored."

Ugh. That is not what one wants to hear when they are seeking medicative assistance to overcome the anxiety induced by weight restoration! I wonder if there is an anti-anxiety medicine that helps with the anxiety induced by anxiety medicines...?

In other news, I did successfully make it through my first weekend on campus... and not only did I survive Saturday, but I even smiled! The water has always been an essential source of bliss and balance in my life; thus, this past week of dryness has done nothing to boost my mood. That was, until Saturday! Now, admittedly, the center's "pool" might better be described as an enlarged puddle, but pathetic as it is, plunging into its icy cold waters was just what I needed to wash away a bit of my medicine head and heavy heart. So, as I recount the week post-plunge, I must admit, though I am not particularly happy here, I can't claim complete misery either. The epiphany tucked away in that admission is an essential one. I'm finally realizing that part of recovery is accepting that we are not supposed to be particularly happy in treatment. We are supposed to be strengthening our resolve by working through the pain so that we can enjoy life on the other side.

Godspeed,
Ryan

DAY 15

Dear Journal,

Today I awoke with that all-too-common paralyzing sense of panic. My weight is down, I get dizzy when I stand up, and the only thing scarier than the thought of staying in a program that is making me sicker is my fear of what I would do if I left it. Damnit! What happened? I had things all figured out. I was going to enroll in a magical month-long retreat at a resort-style residential center in the hills of Hollywood and come out peaceful, purposeful and even a little plumper. Well, I've been in Hollywood for 15 days now, and my inability to surrender to treatment has taken a significant physical and emotional toll on me. Ed is not only speaking louder than ever, but he is shouting – and my morning exercise impulses and snack-skipping schemes have only intensified as a result. The reality is, I cannot yet claim that I want to get better. True, I want to *be* better, but the process of getting better is still too scary for me to fully submit to. In all honesty, I feel like I've lost sight of what "better" even is.

Yesterday, we had our weekly weigh-in with the nutritionist and, thanks to the combination of that damn staircase and my disproportioned and unenforced meals, I have lost five pounds in my attempt to gain ten. Worse yet, I can't pass the blame off to anyone – it's my fault. I feel incredibly alone. True, many addicts and anorexics live on campus, but anxiety, introspection and my anorexic inclination toward self-isolation has robbed me of the ability to be present with anyone other than you and good ol' Ed. So, here I sit, alone, scribbling my fears of the future on a personified piece of paper, dreading the dinner that awaits me in the dining room.

Fear must have been in the air today because it turned into the subject of the morning's group session, as well as the topic of my personal poetic endeavors. The staff here can be a little obsessed with acronyms (those little literary epithets formed from the letters of a word), but the three that they provided to depict the otherwise paralyzing emotion hit home. So, here you have it, my poetic piece on *Fear*, based on the acronyms shared by today's clinical speaker:

FEAR...

An emotion only to be experienced – undefined and misunderstood;
A paralysis of the soul and body that can stiffen one's spirit like wood.
Fight or flight, we react with fright at the sound that its single syllable emits,
But what if our past pains and traumas we were able to forget?

Three acronystic strands – all braided into one;
We alone choose our response – whether to face our fears or run.
Three means of interpretation – three reactions to a call:

F – fuck	F – face	F – false
E – everything	E – emotions	E – evidence
A – and	A – and	A – appearing
R – run	R – recover	R – real

A dance, indeed disordered, and darkened by premonitions of our fall,
Running from our foe leaves us nothing but fatigued,
Because our fears are fast and follow us – our spirits left besieged.
So, when you find yourself faced with fear, you know just what to do,
Face your emotions and recover from the false reality that fear ensues.

Ah, yes - poetry. How fun!
I love rhyming words, but now, it appears, I am done.
So, with that poem I close this journal entry,
But I promise to be back before the turning of the century,

In amiable and obnoxious iambic pentameter,
Ryan

DAY 20

Dear Journal,

Today I told my therapist that I was leaving. Actually, after a week of debilitating indecisiveness, today I told myself that I was leaving... and my therapist happened to be listening in. These past five days have been some of the hardest in recent memory. That is a powerful statement, given the dismal year that my disorder has caused. And as much as I would love to blame the program for not working, today I had to admit to myself that it was I who wasn't doing the work!

I can't help but feel frustrated with myself. That said, this little residential re-run of mine did prove that my variety of disorder doesn't seem to respond well to traditional models of treatment. Does that mean I am hopeless? I sure hope not! What it does mean is that I am going to have to take a lot more responsibility than I have taken thus far for my own recovery. Does it mean that traditional models are flawed? No, but it does demonstrate just how different our disorders can be. Heck, maybe this little book of mine will make it mainstream some day and push providers to be a little less prescriptive in their programming... and/or push patients to be a bit more proactive in their recovery.

As for me? Well, I have a lot of work to do, but I am glad to be able to share the trials and tribulations of the process with the world in the hope that my detours might direct others in their personal journeys. I'll close out this entry with just that: hope. Hope that I can stay motivated. Hope that I can remember how unpleasant being in treatment is and use it as motivation to stay out of residential care in the future. Hope that the six-hour drive back to Santa Cruz will be filled with sunny skies, a salty sea breeze and maybe an epiphany or two. Finally, in awareness that "hope" can indeed "be a dangerous thing", I hope that these past three weeks of pain have purpose beyond just me.

Ryan

DAY 21

Dear Journal,

    I have thoroughly enjoyed playing pen pal with you over the course of these computer-free weeks; however, for as healthy a habit as journaling might be, I don't foresee picking up a pencil all too often now that I have entered back into society. That said, I couldn't close out our time together without one final entry.

    I tried my damnedest to stay out of my head during yesterday's drive back to Santa Cruz. I created a makeshift microphone out of a banana that I'd snagged from the breakfast cart and engaged in miles upon miles of car karaoke, but even my vexing vocals couldn't silence my thoughts. However, for once, that didn't turn out all that bad! Why's that? Well, because yesterday's thoughts weren't too scary. Instead, with the ocean to my left, that painstaking program in my rearview and nothing but open road before me, I found myself speeding forward along highway 1 in route to recovery.

    I had driven nearly three hours in this state of introspective peacefulness before, all of a sudden, something scary finally did occur. My stomach began to growl! *Uh-oh! What am I going to do? I am hungry! I am feeling hunger. This is it,* I thought. I had reached the first fork on post-residential recovery road, and I had a choice to make. *Do I steer toward relapse or recovery?*

I had eaten a decent breakfast that morning and I felt a bit uncomfortable about trusting my hunger cues now that lunch was lingering. In the past, I would force myself to forgo the midday meal, knowing that I'd be stuck in a car, sedentary and seat-belted, all afternoon. However, as I've already alluded, the past was in my rearview. So, in a moment of resilience, I flipped on my turn signal and veered right toward recovery, which took the form of a small roadside deli.

Not a crumb left! I ate both pieces of bread, the entire mound of roast beef, and even the heaping serving of horseradish sauce that complimented it – despite it being mixed with my nutritional nemesis: mayonnaise! Moreover, I enjoyed it!

I can do this. I can fix myself! It was with a satisfied stomach that I came to accept that these past weeks have not broken me, but rather they have helped me see my brokenness. I have spent nearly three decades destroying myself, but now, faced with the task of putting the pieces back together, I finally feel that I'm starting to understand myself. And not simply understand myself, but love myself. And not simply love myself, but love myself enough to give myself the gift of nourishment and rest.

Godspeed,
Ryan

CHAPTER 29

THE ROAD GOES ON FOREVER, BUT THIS BOOK MUST COME TO AN END

Where am I...?

Physically, I am standing at my desk in Santa Cruz, California, with my trusty pooch curled up at my feet, a blanket of fog lingering outside my window, a cup of dandelion root tea steaming at my side, and a slightly embarrassing – yet altogether dance-worthy – 90s hip-hop station streaming from my smart speaker. As for my whereabouts in terms of recovery? Well, like the title of that famous Sir Elton John song, "I'm Still Standing"!

Nearly a year has passed since that residential blooper in West Hollywood, and during that time, I have learned a lot. For example, I mention the tea I am sipping not merely because I enjoy typing the word "dandelion," but because I recently discovered that my coffee addiction was, more accurately, a means of injecting myself with liquid anxiety. As for the poor taste in music? What can I say? I've found it helpful and rather enjoyable to dance away the once-dreaded disordered details of my days. I have even substituted my painstaking, perspiration-inducing gym workouts with dance class!

"Just how many cups of coffee do you drink in a day, Ryan?" My integrative specialist looked up accusingly while reviewing my adrenal function lab report.

"Um... two."

"Just two?"

I cringed before confessing that those *two cups* were each double French-pressed, 16-ounce, freeze-dried-coffee-enhanced mugs of caffeinated mud, which I would sip while snacking on the roasted espresso beans that I had started using to add crunch to my morning yogurt.

"That's what I thought." She shifted the screen of her computer so that I could see the graphic representation of my kookiness. "Your cortisol levels are, quite literally, off the charts."

I'll be damned if she wasn't telling the truth! The squiggles depicting my stress hormones were so far out of the standard range that she had to modify the screen's settings so we could see them.

"Remember how you told me that it felt like you were living in a constant state of panic?"

"Yeah."

"With cortisol levels as high as this, you are! Your body is starved, strained and scared. And adding caffeine into the mix only further fuels the fight-or-flight response that you're feeling."

I knew what was coming next... I also knew that I didn't want to hear it.

"Your body is crying out for rest and nutrition. It is exhausted – and exhaustion can be anxiety-inducing for a compulsive exerciser who feels the constant need to fight it. However, by addressing your anxiety and exhaustion with caffeine, you're simply sending your body deeper into panic." She paused to make sure I was still paying attention. "Think of it this way: If a caveman came across a cougar in the woods, what would he do?"

"Run away?" I didn't know much about cougars, cave people or cortisol, but I figured this was the most logical response.

"Exactly. That is because, at the sight of the cougar, his mind would send a signal to his body, via the release of cortisol, that he was in danger. In response, his adrenaline levels would spike, giving him the burst of energy that he would need to flee. This is a natural human defense mechanism, and quite helpful when fleeing from scary animals; however, that quick burst of energy is not sustainable. If the caveman were to continue to scramble, his body would eventually run out of fuel. His heart would grow weak, his adrenaline would dwindle to anxiety, and he would collapse, left to be cougar food. Sound familiar?"

I nodded.

"You're going to have to choose whether to rest and restrict your caffeine consumption, or collapse and get consumed by a disordered cougar named Ed."

Well, I must admit that it wasn't a pretty breakup, but after a month-long headache, I managed to distance myself from coffee enough that my anxiety started to subside, and my eyes began to open all the way without needing chemical support.

This may seem like an inconsequential climax to this writing project; however, I share it to show how something so simple as decaffeinating one's day can pave the path for a more peaceful recovery journey. And, decaffeinated dandelion tea wasn't the only discovery in these past few months…

"Well, Ryan, I must admit. Yours is one of the more interesting of the autism cases that I have examined."

"Autistic? But I'm a 38-year-old talkative guy. Isn't autism a socially awkward childhood thing?"

Let me backtrack a bit. In response to my most recent failed attempt at residential treatment, I'd been encouraged by several therapists to engage in an intensive psychiatric evaluation process to get a firmer grasp on just what kind of *kooky* it was that I was confronting. Throughout my 30-odd years of existence, I'd been haphazardly labeled "obsessive compulsive," "anorexic," "attention deficit" and a host of other things, but up to this point, I'd never undergone a professional diagnostic screening. Until now, that is.

"That's a common misconception, but from what you have told me about your childhood, it doesn't seem like this is anything new. The only thing that has changed is that you've outgrown your ability to accept yourself for who you are – and you've exhausted yourself attempting to be the person who you feel the world wants you to be."

I could write an entire second book about what the weeks following this autism diagnosis revealed, but for now, take this as an incentive to look beyond the obvious when exploring the roots of your disorder. And remember, a diagnosis, at best, is simply a label; however, my new *label* is helping me understand (and accept) an array of otherwise absurd (and embarrassing) idiosyncrasies, such as my need to adhere to the same detailed daily routine, my over-sensitivity to sensory stimulation, my anxiety around physical intimacy that has ended almost all of my past relationships, and the fact that – despite seeing myself as too skinny – I continue to restrict because I love the sensation of starvation. It helped to explain why, when I do eat, I have always done so in a very meditative, meticulous and preferably private way. It has helped explain why residential care was more traumatic than it was therapeutic – and why exposure therapy never worked with my OCD. It's because I don't have OCD, and you can't expose away your autism!

"You don't have 'compulsions' as much as you have rituals, Ryan." The psychiatrist gave me a quick look-over before continuing. "And you are certainly not obsessively clean or exemplary well kept!" He laughed. "A compulsion is a repetitious act, done out of fear or superstition, that often increases one's anxiety. Someone with OCD gets more anxious as they continue to wash their hands. A ritual, on the other hand, is an activity that an individual does to provide comfort and relieve their anxiety. You live a life of repetition and ritual, not obsessive compulsiveness." He paused. "As for the social thing… you're right! You are incredibly social. So much so that you seem to lack the ability to stop talking or tune down your volume."

Hmm. Okay, I thought. *I'm autistic… but what does that mean?*

It means that I can move one step closer to accepting myself for who I am, one step closer to loving myself. It means that you, too, might want to look into the neurodiversity of your disorder because, as recent studies are now revealing, about 20 to 30 percent of eating disorder cases are now being linked to an underlying, often undiagnosed, autism spectrum disorder.

***

So, once more: Where am I?

Well, I'm an autistic, anorexic, slightly odd 38-year-old guy plodding along his own unique path of recovery. I am not yet recovered, nor do I claim there is truly such a thing; however, my spirit and body are on the mend. My weight is not restored, but it is trending upward. My body is not healed, but I am starting to allow myself to feel my body and emotions again. My days might not all be lined with daffodils, but they are not all disordered either – and I have slowed down enough to stop and smell the flowers that brighten my path.

As such, I am exactly where I need to be. I'm encouraged. And it has been a long time since I have felt optimistic. Recovery is a journey, a dance between physiology and psychiatry, meditation and medication, solitude and sociality, nutrition and rest. It is a dynamic dance, one during which we must remain intentional and attentive. It is a dance that we must practice daily if we hope to remain graceful. And grace means forgiveness, an unconditional forgiveness of oneself and others. Grace is a dance that requires a lightness of the soul. It means finding your rhythm in recovery – not pushing the pace, but always pushing yourself.

We must learn to dance! The not-so-serious scientist Albert Einstein, who earlier defined "insanity" for us, agreed with me. As he put it, "We dance for laughter, we dance for tears, we dance for madness, we dance for fears, we dance for hope, we dance for screams, we are the dancers, we create the dreams."

So, start dancing and dreaming! Dream of a non-disordered life, and don't be afraid to do so with open eyes!

I am not recovered. I'm not a victim. I'm a fighter. I may be cracked, but I'm picking up the broken parts of myself. I won't allow Ed to manipulate my mind. I'm a survivor, and I'm still seeking the self-acceptance and playful perspective that I held as a kid – the kid that existed before Ed ever entered the scene. The kid who laughed loudly and whose love of life was uncorrupted by the traumas of an otherwise crazy world. The kid who ate peanut butter-covered bananas as a midmorning treat without getting tripped up by the calorie count on the back of the jar. The kid who looked forward to lounging on the couch while watching Saturday morning cartoons. The kid who awoke every morning with excitement, not anxiety. The kid who lived a life of curiosity, not compulsivity. The kid who ended his sentences in question marks instead of periods and approached life's challenges as adventures. The kid who saw himself as a superhero in a world untainted by words such as "cancer," "disorder," "doubt," "fear" or "worry." This is the same inner child who exists within each of our un-disordered souls – and my hope is that you, too, can reacquaint yourself with yours!

So, where are YOU?

Recovery is a lifelong journey, but it is possible to enjoy life while we plod along its path. Remember that we were recovered far before we were ever ill. We were born free of the fears and false beliefs of Ed – and as such, our imprisonment is self-imposed. We make the rules. We pick the path. We can dream of a life that we want to live, as we can handle the responsibility to create it.

We have a choice between submitting, surviving or thriving – between living in passive observance or experiencing life. So, wherever you are on your journey, know that we are still standing. It may not always feel that way, but that's because you are battling a disorder bent on fucking with your ability to feel.

Sitting alone with my thoughts during that latest round of residential care, I couldn't help but mourn all the things on which I felt that I was missing out: unhindered happy hours with friends, curling up on the couch without worrying about the workout I wasn't doing, or sharing dessert with a date. However, the reality is that we haven't missed out on anything yet! True, we may not be fully enjoying any of these things in the present, but what if, instead of getting down about what we think we're missing, we got excited about all the things that we have to look forward to in the future? Of course, that is dependent on deciding that you want a future!

I wrote this book as a means of making sense of my insanity and putting to paper a bunch of otherwise undefinable emotions. I also wrote this book as an incentive for you to write your own! Take that as you may, either literally or figuratively. Regardless, remember that your story is not only essential, but you are worthy of sharing it. Our stories are all intertwined, so know that you are never alone – no matter how isolated Ed wants you to feel. If perusing the previous pages helped to prove that, then my purpose has been fulfilled.

Trust in yourself and seek an essence of joy and gratitude in every passing shower because dancing in the rain is the best way to navigate life's storms. Be content with who you are, but never complacent with where you are. Accept yourself because you were meant for something beautiful! You are beautiful! You are powerful! You are lovable! You are loved. Finally, you are not disordered. We are not disordered. We are divine.

I didn't know how to end this book when I started it, but I have come to realize that this is because it was not meant to end. Thus, despite my earlier encouragement to approach life with a question mark instead of a period, in this instance, I feel as though an ellipsis is in order. So, it is with an adventurous spirit, an open-ended ellipsis and the wisdom of *Peter Pan*'s creator J.M. Barrier that I bless your journey with "faith, trust, and pixie dust" − because, as the author famously said, "To live would be an awfully great adventure…"

The End…
Or the beginning…

ACKNOWLEDGEMENTS

There are many magical people who have kept me moving forward during some really, really hard times. My amazing dog, who is currently curled up at my feet, has been a trusty sidekick despite my slips. My magnificent mommy (and yes, I still call her "mommy" at age 37) has remained a steadfast, strong and loving source of support as I strive to take steps forward (and occasionally backwards). My sister, who pulls me out of my panic attacks when I flood her phone on my so-deemed "disorder days." My amazing network of friends, whose acceptance of me has never been conditional upon their understanding me – because Lord knows I don't understand myself!

And, of course, my faith. Because whether we call that cloud in the sky upon whom we cast our prayers God, Krishna, Allah or any other epithet, the simple act of having faith in something larger than ourselves (and that obnoxious eating disorder named Ed) is essential. Thus, my faith in God and the relationship that I hold with her is the reason that I am still alive. And yes, as an ordained Presbyterian minister, I happen to feel more comfortable conversing with the feminine form of a genderless God.

Last, but certainly not least… I acknowledge you! Moreover, I thank you! I thank you for opening your heart to my story because it is through sharing our stories that we put purpose to the pain we experience on this disordered planet called Earth. So, thank you. Thank you for giving me purpose. Thank you for being you. Thank you for wanting to be more than the you that your disorder wants you to be. THANK YOU FOR BEING BEAUTIFUL!

ABOUT CHERISH EDITIONS

Cherish Editions is a bespoke self-publishing service for authors of mental health, well-being and inspirational books.

As a division of Trigger Publishing, the UK's leading independent mental health and well-being publisher, we are experienced in creating and selling positive, responsible, important and inspirational books, which work to de-stigmatize the issues around mental health and improve the mental health and well-being of those who read our titles.

Founded by Adam Shaw, a mental health advocate, author and philanthropist, and leading psychologist Lauren Callaghan, Cherish Editions aims to publish books that provide advice, support and inspiration. We nurture our authors so that their stories can unfurl on the page, helping them to share their uplifting and moving stories.

Cherish Editions is unique in that a percentage of the profits from the sale of our books goes directly to leading mental health charity Shawmind, to deliver its vision to provide support for those experiencing mental ill health.

Find out more about Cherish Editions by visiting cherisheditions.com or joining us on:
Twitter @cherisheditions
Facebook @cherisheditions
Instagram @cherisheditions

Cherish
EDITIONS

ABOUT SHAWMIND

A proportion of profits from the sale of all Trigger books go to their sister charity, Shawmind, also founded by Adam Shaw and Lauren Callaghan. The charity aims to ensure that everyone has access to mental health resources whenever they need them.

Find out more about the work Shawmind do by visiting shawmind.org or joining them on:
   Twitter @Shawmind_
   Facebook @ShawmindUK
   Instagram @Shawmind_

Your Local Mental Health & Wellbeing Charity

CPSIA information can be obtained
at www.ICGtesting.com
Printed in the USA
LVHW031601200423
744793LV00004B/630

9 781913 615987